Thomas Jefferson's Italian and Italian-Related Books in the History of Universal Personal Rights

An Overview

Linda L. Carroll

BORDIGHERA PRESS
NEW YORK, NEW YORK

Robert Viscusi Essay Series
Volume 1

The Robert Viscusi Essay Series is dedicated to the long essay. It intends to publish those studies that are longer than the traditional journal-length essay and yet shorter than the traditional book-length manuscript.

ISBN 978-1-59954-144-0
Library of Congress Control Number: 2019937313

BORDIGHERA PRESS
John D. Calandra Italian American Institute
25 West 43rd Street, 17th Floor
New York, NY 10038

To Bruce, husband and adventuresome companion
in the quest for knowledge and understanding.

"We hold these truths to be self-evident, that all men are created equal, that they are endowed by their Creator with certain inalienable rights, that among these are Life, Liberty, and the pursuit of Happiness."

"[T]u vedrai noi d'una massa di carne tutti la carne avere e da uno medesimo creatore tutte l'anime con iguali forze, con iguali potenze, con iguali vertù create. La vertù primieramente noi, che tutti nascemmo e nasciamo iguali, ne distinse..."

["[Y]ou will see that we all have flesh from the same mass of flesh and from the same creator all have souls created with equal forces, with equal powers, and with equal capabilities. Capability is the first thing that distinguished us, who all have been born and are born equal..."]

Giovanni Boccaccio, *Decameron*

TABLE OF CONTENTS

THOMAS JEFFERSON'S ITALIAN AND ITALIAN-RELATED BOOKS IN THE HISTORY OF UNIVERSAL PERSONAL RIGHTS

AN OVERVIEW

Introduction

As Thomas Jefferson acknowledged, the concepts advanced in the Declaration of Independence that he largely drafted embodied "'the common sense of the subject'" rather than "'new ideas'." He elaborated: "'Neither aiming at originality of principle or sentiment, nor yet copied from any particular and previous writing, it was intended to be an expression of the American mind'."[1] The Declaration's concepts epitomized the eighteenth-century flowering of notions such as universal human equality and rights resulting from millennia of European development that began in ancient Greece and that included important contributions from Italian thinkers of the Middle Ages through the Enlightenment. Jefferson's awareness of this tradition is represented in the books that he chose for his library, especially relevant because, as James Gilreath and D. L. Wilson perceived, for Jefferson "[u]nderstanding the historical dimension of any subject was crucial to a meaningful comprehen-

---

[1] Quoted and discussed in Marie Kimball, *Jefferson The Road to Glory 1773 to 1776* (New York: Coward-McCann, 1943) 305-306.

sion of the present." Trevor Colbourn notes that "Jefferson
shared with certain European contemporaries common
attitudes toward history and its uses, and both his ideas of
the past and his employment of those ideas contribute sub-
stantially to our understanding of Jefferson and his revolutionary generation.... In part, he studied history as an ex-
tension of political experience and a guide to the perfecti-
ble future through the errors of the blemished past. But he
also studied history for a model of that future ... the character of Jefferson's reading habits, his peculiar preferences
and comments on them, can and do inform powerfully on
his own thinking." Moreover, Jefferson's interests being
universal, he read avidly on a vast range of topics and applied the lessons gained to an equally vast range of endeav-
ors. According to Gilreath and Wilson, "Jefferson's reading
seems to have informed so many of his activities that close
attention to the books in his library offers useful insights to
students of almost any aspect of his multifaceted career." In
the words of Adrienne Koch, "Since his library was the
product of extraordinary devotion and, as he said, 'hand-
picked', it is a valuable index to his intellectual attach-
ments.[2] And Jefferson had a civic goal for his reading. Gilreath and Wilson note, "Jefferson constantly sifted through
world literature seeking those books that contained infor-

[2] James Gilreath and Douglas L. Wilson, eds., *Thomas Jefferson's Library. A Catalog with the Entries in His Own Order* (Washington, D.C.: Library of Congress, 1989) 3, 9-10, Koch quoted 4; H. Trevor Colbourn, "Thomas Jeffer-son's Use of the Past," *The William and Mary Quarterly*, 3rd series, 15 (1958): 56-70, quotations 56-57, 59; see also Karl Lehmann, *Thomas Jefferson Ameri-can Humanist* (Chicago: University of Chicago Press, 1965) 71-76.

mation and ideas that might benefit his country. This catalog [of Jefferson's library] presents the distillation of the
efforts by one of America's leading intellectuals to organize
the knowledge of the Old World so as to make it useful for
the New ... his library not only offers a key to his own
thinking but also symbolizes an admirable and important
part of the cultural tradition of the American society he
envisioned and helped to found."

The subjects of the current essay are the history of Italian thought on universal natural rights and self-governance
and sources contributing to it as represented in Jefferson's
library; its congruity with his views prior to 1776 and with
the pre-Enlightenment and Enlightenment thinkers such as
Hobbes, Montesquieu, Sidney, and Locke cited as his usual inspirations; and Jefferson's application and further development of such thinking. Research demonstrates that
they are subjects meriting greater attention than heretofore
received.[3] In Karl Lehmann's perceptive description of the
relationship between Jefferson's thought and ancient
sources, "The eighteenth century style of Jefferson's men-
tality and the all-pervasive intellectual climate of his age
make it difficult, if not impossible, to say in each case
whether the articulation of a specific viewpoint was bor-
rowed by him from an antique source or whether he simp-
ly found confirmation in such sources. Wherever I have
pointed out and documented the relationship between Jef-

---

[3] On the need for broader and deeper studies of Jefferson's library/libraries, see Charles B. Sanford, *Jefferson and His Library* (Hamden, CT: Archon Books, 1977) 8-9.

ferson and such sources, I mean to leave this question open to discussion."[4] The approach here will be similar. Because Jefferson's books deal chiefly with issues of equality, justice, and rights, the essay will in a sense provide the complement to *The Machiavellian Moment*'s study of liberty and control that J. G. A. Pocock called for in a recent afterward.[5] The essay will first give evidence of Jefferson's knowledge of Italian, then present the history of the questions and note similarities. Research was conducted in the Library of Congress on Jefferson's copies or, for lost volumes, a copy of the same edition.[6] Knowledge of Jefferson's libraries and their contents over the course of his life is necessarily incomplete because of the vicissitudes from which they suffered. Translations unless otherwise noted are by the present author.

Illustrative of Jefferson's characterization of his words as summarizing common ideas is the example of his Italian neighbor in Virginia, Philip (Filippo) Mazzei, who about two years earlier had written "All men are by nature equally free and independent. Their equality is necessary in order to set up a free government. Every man must be the equal of any other in natural rights."[7] Jefferson translated such

---

[4] Lehmann, xvi.

[5] J. G. A. Pocock, *The Machiavellian Moment. Florentine Political Thought and the Atlantic Republican Tradition* (Princeton: Princeton University Press, 2003) 553-83.

[6] I express my deep gratitude to Chief of the Rare Book and Special Collections Division Mark Dimunation and Eric Frazier of the Division for their constant, generous and invaluable assistance with the project.

[7] Quoted from Filippo Mazzei, *Philip Mazzei: Selected Writings and Correspondence*, ed. Margherita Marchione, Stanley J. Idzerda, and S. Eugene Scalia, 3

early political writings of Mazzei for a time, until he felt that Mazzei had developed sufficient language skills to produce the English version on his own.

While Mazzei's wording in these texts has been considered a likely influence on Jefferson's, it has not been recognized that core elements of the concepts and phrasing appeared in one of the most widely-read Italian works of the early Renaissance, Giovanni Boccaccio's *Decameron* (quoted above). Mazzei requested two copies of the text in a letter of January 7, 1775 to Giovanni Fabbroni (whom Jefferson would attempt unsuccessfully to hire as his children's tutor three years later) in a list of books to be sent to him.[8] It is tempting to wonder if the second copy might be the 1751 edition that Jefferson held in his library.[9] Another

---

vols. (Prato: Edizioni del Palazzo, 1983) [hereafter *Philip Mazzei*, all references are to vol. 1], vol. 1, 68 (translation by the editors from a later Italian version); see also Howard R. Marraro, ed. and trans., "Philip Mazzei on American Political, Social, and Economic Problems," *The Journal of Southern History* 15 (1949): 354-78, esp. 354-58 on Jefferson and Mazzei, the texts involved, and Jefferson's role in the translation of Mazzei's early political writings. Because, as both editors note (70 and 355 respectively), there are no known original issues of the *Virginia Gazette* of the period 1774-75 in which Mazzei first published these views under the pseudonym 'Orlando furioso', the sentences are excerpted from a version that Mazzei later published in Italian. On Mazzei in colonial Virginia, see also Philip Mazzei, *Memoirs of the Life and Peregrinations of the Florentine Philip Mazzei 1730-1816*, trans. Howard R. Marraro (New York: Columbia University Press, 1942) [hereafter Mazzei, *Memoirs*] 197-223.

[8] *Philip Mazzei: Selected Writings*, 71; Kevin J. Hayes, *The Road to Monticello. The Life and Mind of Thomas Jefferson* (New York: Oxford University Press, 2008) 211.

[9] See E. Millicent Sowerby, *Catalogue of the Library of Thomas Jefferson*, 5 vols. (Washington: The Library of Congress, 1952), vol. 4, 440, #4321; no purchase information was available in Jefferson's records and the volume is no longer extant. While the stated place of publication is Amsterdam, renowned for its intellectual freedom, such claims were often made falsely to avoid the censor for books actually printed in Italy.

potential source was *Della lingua Toscana di Benedetto Buommatei*, a renowned grammar of Italian first published in 1623 and republished many times, that Jefferson owned. It traces the history of the development of the Italian language through literature and learned societies and illustrates language structures with quotations from literary texts, especially Boccaccio's *Decameron*.[10]

As is evident in Jefferson's translations of Mazzei's writings, the Italian language did not pose an obstacle to his reading of texts. He developed his knowledge of it early, assisted by his command of French and Latin and by his precision in linguistic matters. In 1764, Jefferson purchased a number of Italian books: an Italian-English dictionary, Francesco Guicciardini's *Istoria d'Italia*, Enrico Caterino Davila's *Istoria delle guerre di Francia* (which in 1771 he recommended to a friend as part of a gentleman's basic library), and Machiavelli's *Opera* in two volumes.[11] He studied Italian during his early years, in 1761 reading Pietro Chiari's translation of *Tom Jones* and in 1767 recording for the first time the name of his planned home, Monticello, taken from the Italian text of Andrea Palladio's *Quattro libri dell'Architettura*.[12] He delighted

---

[10] Benedetto Buommattei, *Della lingua Toscana di Benedetto Buommatei* (Venice, 1735), Sowerby, vol. 5, 91 #4804; no information on its purchase is available.
[11] Kimball, 77, 106.
[12] Hayes, 68; Guido Beltramini, "Jefferson and Palladio," in *Jefferson and Palladio. Constructing a New World*, Centro Internazionale di Studi di Architettura Andrea Palladio, exh. cat. Vicenza, Palladio Museum 19 September 2015 - 28 March 2016 (Vicenza: Centro Internazionale di Studi di Architettura Andrea Palladio; Milan: Officina Libraria, 2015) 21-37, 23-24; Beltramini notes that Jefferson probably used the Giacomo Leoni triple-language (English, Italian,

Mazzei's Tuscan workmen by addressing them in their native language when Mazzei consulted with him on agricultural matters in 1775.[13] For the Italian books that he entered into his hand-written catalogue of those to be consigned to the Library of Congress, he created his own abbreviated titles in Italian.[14] Finally, as exemplified by the edition of Palladio's master work, the most important Italian works in his library had editions in other languages that Jefferson commanded, some of which he owned, or were much discussed in the intellectual circles of the time.

Mazzei's 1775 book order, quoted here in full, contained twelve entries; all by Italian authors with the sole exception of Virgil, they were well-known works of literature, history, the social sciences, and the natural sciences relevant to agriculture. Edoardo Tortarolo, having found evidence that Mazzei ordered valued Italian texts for various American friends including James Madison, considers that most of them were for Jefferson.[15]

> 2 Guicciardini, *Storia d'Italia*, latest edition
> 2 Davila, *Guerre civili*, assuming that the London edition is not the best,
> 2 Dante, commentary by Venturi

---

and French) edition. For the custom of reading texts simultaneously in the original language and English, see Jason Lawrence, *'Who the devil taught thee so much Italian?' Italian Language Learning and Literary Imitation in Early Modern England* (Manchester and New York: Manchester University Press, 2005).

[13] Mazzei, *Memoirs*, 192-93.

[14] These improvised titles are quoted by Sowerby in her catalogue.

[15] Edoardo Tortarolo, *Illuminismo e Rivoluzione: Biografia politica di Filippo Mazzei* (Milan: Franco Angeli, 1986) 42-43.

2 Boccaccio, *Decamerone*

1 Cocchi, *Bagni di Pisa*

2 Marchese Beccaria, *Dei delitti e delle pene*

2 Ditto, *On commerce*

2 Redi, *Opere*

1 Tasso, *Gerusalemme*

1 Vergil's *Aeneid* trans. by Father Ant. Ambrogi, S.J., Rome edition. It is to be had at Carlieri's

All of Fontana's brochues

Vasari, *Le vite de' pittori*, with Bottari's notes ...

The book by Signor Carlo Denini, Professor of Eloquence and Belles Lettres at the University of Turin, on literary history, its progress and decadence and causes thereof from the Greeks to our day.[16]

Jefferson's own library included nearly all the titles, although it is not clear when some of them entered it or whether others were lost without record. Those with documented ownership, with publication dates in parentheses, are: Francesco Guicciardini, *Istoria d'Italia* (1738); Enrico Caterino Davila, *Istoria delle guerre civili di Francia* (1745); Dante Alighieri, *La Divina Commedia* (1785); Boccaccio, *Decameron* (1751); Cesare Beccaria, *Dei delitti e delle pene* (pre-1769) and the English translation *An essay on crimes & punishments* (New York, 1809); Francesco Redi, *Esperienze intorno a diverse Cose Naturali e particolarmente quelle, che ci son portate dalle Indie* (1671); Torquato Tasso, *Gerusalemme Liberata* (1763); Virgil, *Aeneid* (1600); Felice Fontana, *Ricerche*

---

[16] Quoted from *Philip Mazzei*, 71 (translation by the editors).

fisiche sopra il veleno della vipera (Lucca, 1767); and Giorgio Vasari, *Delle Vite de' più Eccellenti Pittori, Scultori ed Architetti* in a seventeenth-century presentation edition. He also owned a volume by Antonio Cocchi on marriage (1762) and one on anatomy (1745), though not the title cited by Mazzei.[17]

All the texts were well known and widely read at the time. Moreover, Jefferson, who from childhood read avidly and widely, acquired many more Italian and Italian-influenced works, and on a range of topics whose vastness demonstrates his eclectic tastes and deep erudition.[18] Among them are many that developed the concept of nature-based and therefore universal human equality and the concept that governing authority is held by the human community, two concepts critical to his and other Americans' thought as they moved toward independence.[19] The

[17] See respectively in the Sowerby catalogue: vol. 1, 76 #165 (Guicciardini); vol. 1, 88 #198 (Davila; cf. a title in the Biblioteca Nazionale Marciana of Venice http://polovea.sebina.it/SebinaOpac/Opac.do#5); vol. 4, 435 #4310 (Dante); vol. 4, 440 #4321 (Boccaccio; no longer extant); vol. 3, 21 #2349 (Beccaria) and see page 56 for the Italian edition; vol. 1, 470 #1033 (Redi); vol. 4, 425 #4291 (Tasso); vol. 4, 420 #4280 (Virgil); vol. 1, 473 #1041 (Fontana); vol. 4, 393 #4240 (Vasari); vol. 1, 416 #916 and 451 #997 (Cocchi).

[18] On the vastness of Jefferson's erudition and his passion for books, see Kimball; Sowerby; Lehmann; Colbourn; Gilreath and Wilson; Hayes; Adrienne Koch, "Jefferson and the Pursuit of Happiness," in *Power, Morals, and the Founding Fathers* (Ithaca: Cornell University Press, 1961) 23-49; Sanford; Douglas L. Wilson, "Jefferson's Library," in *Thomas Jefferson: A Reference Biography*, ed. Merrill D. Peterson (New York: Charles Scribner's Sons, 1986) 157-79.

[19] For relevant documents, see Thomas Jefferson, *The Papers of Thomas Jefferson*, ed. Julian P. Boyd, Editor, Lyman H. Butterfield and Mina R. Bryan, Associate Editors (Princeton: Princeton University Press, 1950-), vol. 1 *1760-1776*; subsequent citations will be to this volume with the reference Jefferson, *Papers;* 119-433, esp. 119-20 "Draft of a Declaration of Rights Prepared for the Virginia Convention of August 1774"; 121-37 "Draft of Instructions to the

dates of the texts cover much of the time span of these concepts' development from their roots in ancient Greece and Rome, to the Middle Ages, the Renaissance, and the Enlightenment. Because Jefferson's Italian and Italian-related books have not yet been systematically included in studies of the sources of the views expressed in the Declaration of Independence, the present work will discuss those most relevant to his thought in the period preceding its drafting. Consideration will proceed in chronological order to trace the concepts' evolution and diffusion and include some that, while not present in Jefferson's library, influenced those that were.

Among the holdings, as meticulously catalogued by E. Millicent Sowerby, those most relevant form three large semantic categories: personal rights (especially regarding personal conduct, including non-canonical forms of marriage), political rights of individuals and communities (especially norms of broad-based participation in governance and the view that the governing authority over a given community originated in the community itself), the structure and functioning of states (including the freedom of civil states from control by religious authorities).

Virginia Delegates in the Continental Congress" also known as "A Summary View..."; 177-82 "Jefferson's Annotated Copy of Franklin's Proposed Articles of Confederation"; 337-66 Jefferson's drafts of the Virginia Constitution; 413-33 the drafts of the Declaration of Independence.

Origins of Western Notions of Equality and Freedom

The earliest concepts of the equal rights of all human beings based on a common human nature developed in ancient Greece, in the philosophical works of the Stoics and in the literary-theatrical works of Lucian of Samosata and Euripides.[20] As explicated by Marcia Colish, Stoic thought emphasized unity and nature: the unity of the human mind and body, the unity of all humans, and the unity of humans with the rest of nature, a unity from which human equality flows. "In their common possession of reason, a fragment of the divine *logos*, all men by nature are equal."[21] Jefferson's familiarity with this thought is evidenced by his copying into his early literary commonplace book of Euripides's statement, "Nature gave men the law of equal rights."[22] Extending the concept in literary and performative terms, Lucian of Samosata adapted the philosophical form of the dialogue to his stagings in works that questioned the legitimacy of the accumulation of political power by a small number. Signally, his *Tyrannicida* justifies ridding the populace of a tyrannical ruler and his descent line to free the people from violent oppression and to restore democracy.

---

[20] For the influence of Stoic and Epicurean thought on Jefferson's views, see e.g. Koch, 31-32; Charles A. Miller, *Jefferson and Nature: An Interpretation* (Baltimore: The Johns Hopkins University Press, 1988), esp. 23, 99ff.

[21] See Marcia L. Colish, *The Stoic Tradition from Antiquity to the Early Middle Ages*, 2 vols. (Leiden: Brill, 1985) for a comprehensive history; quotation vol. 1, 37.

[22] Thomas Jefferson, *Jefferson's Literary Commonplace Book*, ed. Douglas L. Wilson, The Papers of Thomas Jefferson, Second Series (Princeton: Princeton University Press, 1989) 71, excerpt 122; Lehmann, pp 43-44, 48, 61, 71-73, 76, 84, 94.

Stoic thought developed further in Rome, especially in the thought of Seneca and Cicero. In Colish's words, Seneca saw "the loss of liberty, chastity, or good conscience" as worse than death. Cicero, in "an important and creative accomplishment and one destined to be extremely influential in post-classical legal and political thought," developed the Stoic notion of natural law "as an ethical and cosmic principle into a legal principle to be used as the norm of the legitimacy of the civil law of a given historical community."[23] According to Charles F. Mullett, it was this very formulation that appealed to colonials: "Most frequently cited was Cicero's definition of law as 'the highest reason, instituted in nature, which orders what should be done and prohibits the contrary'."[24]

Christianity amplified notions of equality in seeing all human beings as equal before God and contributed greatly to notions of individual autonomy by introducing the tenet of free will. Civic entities began to benefit from related views in the Middle Ages, as Italian communes developed ideas and structures of self-governance suiting their condition as largely independent of the geographically close overlordship that began to characterize northern Europe with Charlemagne. In the early phases, many Italian villages and even major towns such as Padua had as an authority figure only the local bishop, whose dependence on the population for his defense force was leveraged by laymen to in-

---

[23] Colish, *Stoic Tradition*, vol. 1, 13-158, quotations 49 and 96.
[24] Charles F. Mullett, "Classical Influences on the American Revolution," *The Classical Journal* 35 (1939): 92-104, quotation 102.

crease their power.[25] They developed relatively horizontal forms of government, typically ample governing councils encompassing a significant portion of the male population (*e.g.* all heads of households).[26] Larger towns such as Venice and Florence assumed the form of republics.

With the formation of the new civic entities came new civic needs. The search for legal codes with which to govern them resulted in the twelfth-century revival of Roman law and the codification of canon law in Gratian's Decretum. New civic buildings also arose, signally Padua's aptly-named Palazzo della Ragione (*ragione*'s multiple meanings including 'reason', 'discussion', 'law', and 'accounting'). The largest government building in Europe at the time of its construction in the late twelfth and early thirteenth centuries, it provided ample space for the commune's totemic tribunals and for notarial and commercial functions. As Brian Tierney has demonstrated, legal codifications of equality were accompanied by the "concern with individual intention, individual consent, individual will that characterized twelfth-century culture."[27] Joan Ferrante saw a contribution by the

---

[25] Aldo Checchini, "Comuni rurali padovani," *Nuovo Archivio Veneto* n.s. 18 (1909): 131-84, esp. 143-47, 154-55, 159-62. For lower population creating a demand for work resulting in improved conditions for laborers: Checchini summarizing the views of Gaetano Salvemini; Hermann Rebel, *Peasant Classes. The Bureaucratization of Property and Family Relations Under Early Hapsburg Absolutism 1511-1636* (Princeton: Princeton University Press, 1982).

[26] For the example of Venice, see Thomas F. Madden, *Enrico Dandolo and the Rise of Venice* (Baltimore: The Johns Hopkins University Press, 2003).

[27] Brian Tierney, "Origins of Natural Rights Language: Texts and Contexts, 1150-1250," *History of Political Thought* 10 (1989): 615-46, esp. 625-46, quotation 627; see also the extensive presentation in Brian Tierney, *The Idea of Natural Rights* (Atlanta: Scholar's Press for Emory University, 1997).

period's broad-based economic prosperity to its relatively liberal social norms and personal freedom, including the greater role afforded to women and the willingness to recognize their importance.[28]

In the following century, the concept of nature-based equal rights before the law was developed by Roman and canon lawyers. The rediscovery of the Stoic thought of Aristotle made an important contribution to the effort as theologians, principally Albertus Magnus and his pupil Thomas Aquinas, applied Aristotelian-Stoic notions of equal rights to ethical issues. In the summary of Marcia Colish, "Thomas lays the foundation for a non-ascetic, natural ethics in which reason and the golden mean rule our use of our physical, emotional, and mental endowments. Virtue can bear fruit in all these aspects of our nature. In attaining our natural ends, Thomas holds that we actualize our potentialities naturally. He adds to this generally Aristotelian account the Stoic notion of natural law as right reason, an ethical norm that all human beings can apprehend on their own. From it we derive rationally our natural ethical obligations."[29] Jefferson's knowledge of this strain of European thought is evidenced in his references to Aquinas and to Scotus, as well as his use of

---

[28] Joan M. Ferrante, *Woman as Image in Medieval Literature* (New York and London: Columbia University Press, 1975), esp. 1-15.

[29] Marcia Colish, *Medieval Foundations of the Western Tradition* (New Haven: Yale University Press, 1999) 291-301, quotation 300. See also Riccardo Saccenti, *Debating Medieval Natural Law. A Survey* (Notre Dame: University of Notre Dame Press, 2016).

Thomistic terms.[30]

Contemporaneously and also on the basis of Aristotelian philosophy, notions of the equal right of self-governance were articulated in political theory. According to Brian Tierney, "Throughout the whole medieval period the 'descending' thesis was implicit in the accepted Christian conception of the universe to this extent at least: no one denied that licit dominion came ultimately from God. But from about 1250 onward the problem arose of combining this apparently self-evident doctrine with new versions of the 'ascending' thesis based on the Aristotelian teaching that society and the state were natural to man. In the ensuing discussions, a cluster of ideas emerged that would have a continuous history of development in Western constitutional thought down to the time of Leslie and Locke."[31] The substitution of the 'descending' theory of governance, according to which governing power was bestowed by a supernatural being upon a designated head of the community, with the 'ascending' theory, that governance belongs to the community and is conditionally delegated by it to a governing individual or group, is the core of American developments. Jefferson was aware early on that the ancient Greek colonies in Sicily maintained the tradition of self-governance of their home city-states, al-

---

[30] Lehmann, 61; Thomas Jefferson, "accidental" in letter to James Madison of May 12, 1792 quoted in Lehmann, 83 and see also 'substance' and 'accidents' in his letter to S. Kercheval of July 12, 1816.

[31] Brian Tierney, "Public expediency and natural law: a fourteenth-century discussion on the origins of government and property," in *Authority and Power: Studies on Medieval Law and Government Presented to Walter Ullmann on his Seventieth Birthday,* ed. Brian Tierney and Peter Linehan (Cambridge: Cambridge University Press, 1980) 167-82, quotation 168.

though he refrained from citing this precedent in his 1774 "Summary View of the Rights of British America" "evidently due to tactical considerations which made it advisable to stick to strictly legal British precedent at a time when there was still a hope of preserving the union with the British Crown."[32]

By the early fourteenth century, in Tierney's finding, many thinkers including the influential William of Ockham held the view that, according to natural law and natural reason and supported by a Roman example, the original right to authority over a human community lay within that community itself and not outside of it. For the sake of efficient governance, the community could delegate certain of its powers to specific individuals through an election. Ockham carried notions of individual and collective rights even further, being the first to hold that "the power of rulers was limited by the rights of their subjects," that a community and individuals retained certain rights even after electing a ruler, and that a ruler could be removed for grave wrongs. Moreover, Ockham held that the papacy's powers were even narrower than those of a civil ruler because the office had not been delegated by a human community that had founded it and because the pope was limited in his authority by the liberty of action that God had granted to each individual through free will. Finally, he held that subjects were not required to obey the commands of either a civil or an ecclesiastical authority that ran counter to natural or divine law, or those of a pope

---

[32] Lehmann, 94; cfr. Koch, 38-49.

that were "unjust because they violated the rights of others without fault or cause.' Ockham adduced as justification that "scripture limited papal power by safeguarding the natural and civil rights of the pope's subjects."[33]

Papal infallibility, as Francis Oakley wrote in supporting Tierney's further views, was a "late-medieval invention" of certain Franciscans defending papal "endorsement (1279) of the doctrine of apostolic poverty" and Conciliarism was not "unorthodox ecclesiology of revolutionary vintage" but "an essentially moderate doctrine of unimpeachably orthodox foundations in the cozy respectabilities of the pre-Marsilian era...." Moreover, according to Oakley, the Conciliarists of the early fifteenth century (see also below) held that the body of the faithful had only delegated its authority over itself to the pope to act for the body's good and that if the body perceived the pope acting to subvert or destroy it it could, through representatives, "judge, chastise and even depose the pope."[34] The same principle informs the statement in the Declaration following the one quoted above: "That to secure these rights, Governments are instituted among Men, deriving their just powers from the consent of the governed, — That whenever any Form of Government becomes destructive of these ends, it is the Right of the People to alter or to abolish it, and to institute new

---

[33] Tierney, *Idea*, 181-93, quotations 183, 186, 187.
[34] Francis Oakley, "Religious and Ecclesiastical Life on the Eve of the Reformation," in *Reformation Europe: A Guide to Research*, ed. Steven Ozment (St. Louis: Center for Reformation Research, 1982) 5-32, quotations 15-16; *id.*, "The 'New Conciliarism' and Its Implications: A Problem in History and Hermeneutics," *Journal of Ecumenical Studies* 8 (1971): 815-40, 818-9.

Government..." Jefferson may have been informed of Conciliarism by American Catholics, who espoused it both for their belief that each state should be free and independent and to alleviate the fears of their fellow colonials that they owed allegiance to the pope and that therefore their patriotism could not be trusted. Leaders in this Conciliarist Catholic view and holding it from as early as 1760 were Marylanders Charles Carroll of Carrollton, a fellow Signer, and his second cousins the brothers John and Daniel Carroll. John, a Jesuit, was the first bishop and archbishop of the United States and Daniel, together with Charles, contributed to the writing of the First Amendment and the Maryland state constitution.[35]

Following Aristotle, Ockham also emphasized the role of the community and its function as an instrument of the common good, while holding that it exercised authority only over the actions of the collectivity and not over those of its individual members. This issue was also one of special concern to Jefferson, who was opposed to the Continental Congress's acting on behalf of the individual colonies in matters in which the colonies had not specifically provided prior authorization to the Congress.

Marsilius of Padua, associated with the Italian Ghibelline (imperial) party, developed community rights to the fullest in the *Defensor pacis*, written between 1320 and 1324 in Paris where he had been a professor and rector

---

[35] On American Conciliarism and the Carrolls' role, see Michael D. Breidenbach, "Conciliarism and the American Founding," *William and Mary Quarterly*, 3rd ser. 73 (2016): 467-500.

of the university. Beyond affirming the community's original jurisdiction over itself, he asserted for the first time in
Christian Europe the state's independence from ecclesiastical authority, an independence that Jefferson later noted
among Germanic peoples and the Anglo-Saxons. Quentin
Skinner saw Marsilius as inspired by Aristotle's works,
which provided a "new confidence as well as a new ar-
moury of concepts with which to challenge the orthodox
Augustinian assumption that all governments are imposed
by God's ordinance as a mere remedy for human sinful-
ness."[36] According to Tierney, Marsilius in that same text
first made the "distinction between *ius* as objective law
and *ius* as subjective right."[37] Thus the dual meaning of *ius*
("objective law," *i.e.* the norm through which an external
authority regulates the conduct of an individual or entity,
and "subjective right," *i.e.* the undeniable access of an
individual or entity to self-sustenance and self-governance)
was applied contemporaneously in parallel fashion to the
individual, to the political body, and to the formalized
state. Jefferson, to whom these sources were unavailable,
saw an absence of self-governance in the Continental tradition, which he attributed not only to Roman law but to
the clergy's support for hierarchical governance brought
to England by William the Conqueror and superimposed

---

[36] Quentin Skinner, "Political Philosophy," in *The Cambridge History of Renais-
sance Philosophy*, ed. Charles B. Schmitt and Quentin Skinner (Cambridge:
Cambridge University Press, 1988) 389-452, quotation 396. See also Oakley,
"Religious and Ecclesiastical Life."

[37] Tierney, "Public expediency," 174; Tierney, *Idea*, 108-18, quotation 109.

upon the self-governance notions of the Anglo-Saxons, on which he based Americans' rights to it.[38]

Important breakthroughs in support of individual rights also occurred around 1300 in the cultural realm, including in the role of women. In those years Giotto adorned Padua's Arena Chapel with two fresco cycles—not only the customary life of Jesus, but the first known life cycle of Mary, still the largest and most comprehensive. The cycle complemented her role in the chapel's great west wall fresco of the Last Judgment in which she offers the chapel to her Son, presumably as an inducement to Him to save the soul of Reginaldo (Rainaldo) Scrovegni, a wealthy practitioner of usury and the father of the Enrico who had commissioned it. The frescoes clearly convey Scrovegni's fear that the protection afforded to his father (and likely himself) by riches in this world would not prevent his condemnation by a just God in the next, and that his only hope for salvation lay in converting his fortune to religious ends and having his case pled by the judge's mother.

Reginaldo's profile among usurers was so high that he was chosen by Dante to speak of their sin in his *Divine Comedy* (*Inferno* XVII, vv. 64-75[39]), a text owned by Jefferson. Thus, the equality of all humans makes its first appearance

---

[38] Kimball, 245-48; Colbourn; Lehmann, 95-96, 115.

[39] See James Stubblebine, ed., *Giotto: The Arena Chapel Frescoes* (New York: Norton, 1969), esp. Dorothy C. Shorr, "The Role of the Virgin in Giotto's *Last Judgment*," 169-82 and Ursula Schlegel, "On the Pictorial Program of the Arena Chapel," 182-202; Giuseppe Basile, "Giotto's Pictorial Cycle," in *Giotto. The Frescoes of the Scrovegni Chapel in Padua*, ed. Giuseppe Basile (Milan: Skira; Rome: Istituto Centrale per il Restauro, 2002) 21-39.

contemporaneously in literature and in the figurative arts in God's judgment of all without regard to their place in a hierarchy. Succinctly put, in Dante's scheme, which reflects Catholic teaching, God applies equal justice to each human being in judging his or her actions, and on that basis assigns the soul to one of the three realms of the afterlife.

Several decades later, Boccaccio, who studied law, resumes the secular thread of the earlier jurists in the collection of one hundred *novelle* (tales) entitled *Decameron*. He bases many of them on the tacit assumption that characters possess basic rights which, when their exercise is denied by social authority (either a person or the letter of the law), the characters may themselves claim through ingenious and discreet means. The key to success is appearing to conform to social authority while silently subverting it to meet the spirit of the natural law. To do so, one must avoid alerting others and giving rise to scandal. Thus, for example, in the tale of Zima (III, 5), the wife who is denied legitimate marital pleasures by her husband's travelling to fulfill his political ambitions may take the low-born but personally-refined lover to whom her husband introduced her in his greed to obtain the man's handsome palfrey for free, provided that she do so in a discreetly coded way (by placing a towel in her window).

In the first tale of Day Four, a day dedicated to love that ends tragically, Boccaccio explicitly states the natural law and its equal availability to all in the passage cited above. It is part of a speech by Ghismonda, the daughter of Tancredi, Prince

21

of Salerno, on whom he dotes, waiting until late to fulfill his duty to find her a husband. Shortly after the wedding, Ghismonda's noble husband dies and she returns to her father's house; being still young, she hopes for a second marriage. At Tancredi's failure to respond, she "got the idea of wanting to take, if it were possible, in a hidden way a worthy lover" (si pensò di volere avere, se esser potesse, occultamente un valoroso amante).[40] Having considered the many men at her father's court, she chooses a valet humble of birth but noble of virtues and behavior who has fallen deeply in love with her. She having instructed him on a secret route to her chamber, they meet there frequently. One day her father falls asleep behind a curtain there and witnesses their union. When he calls her to account for it, she emphasizes her youth with its laws and its desires, reminding him that he too had known them. To his vilification of her lover for his low social station, she responds:

> ... you will see that we all have flesh from the same mass of flesh and from the same creator all have souls created with equal forces, with equal powers, and with equal capabilities. Capability is the first thing that distinguished us, who all have been born and are born equal; and those who had the greater share of it and acted were called noble and the rest not noble.
>
> [... tu vedrai noi d'una massa di carne tutti la carne avere e da uno medesimo creatore tutte l'anime con iguali forze, con iguali potenze, con iguali vertù create.

[40] Giovanni Boccaccio, *Decameron*, ed. Vittore Branca, Vol. 4 of *Tutte le opere* (Milan: Mondadori, 1976), IV, 1..

La vertù primieramente noi, che tutti nascemmo e
nasciamo iguali, ne distinse; e quegli che di lei maggior
parte avevano e adoperavano nobili furon detti, e il
rimanente rimase non nobile. (355)]

She concludes that he should mete out to her the same
fate as to her lover, or she will do so herself. Tancredi,
unmoved, has her lover killed; Ghismonda asserts control
over her life in the only way remaining, by ending it.

Ghismonda's statement contains many of the elements of the Declaration's statement: equality based on
common physical humanity, the creator's endowing the
souls of all with the same faculties, freedom of comport-
ment, and self-determination. However, it also unites such
basic equality with the notion of earned social hierarchy; a
similar union characterizes Jefferson's formulations of
"equal moral rights at birth" but varied talents or "potential to develop them" leading to a "natural aristocracy"
and to his distinction, as brilliantly observed by Maurizio
Valsania, of 'nature' as a key to perfectability in himself
but a "constraining and limiting force" in others.[41]

The Development of Notions of Rights and Equality in the Italian Renaissance

Jefferson's library reflects the paucity of fifteenth-cen-
tury Italian texts, followed by their increase in the mature

---

[41] Description of Jefferson's views in Miller, 83-84; Maurizio Valsania, *Jefferson's Body. A Corporeal Biography* (Charlottesville: University of Virginia Press, 2017) 4-5.

Renaissance. Amerigo Vespucci's letters describing the communal and non-acquisitive if cannibalistic cultures of the New World entered his library in a 1745 Italian edition. He owned a 1741 edition of the works of Ludovico Ariosto in the original, published in Venice. Its four volumes collected the complete works expressing the Ferrarese author's conflicted, satirical take on the turmoil of his age in the comic epic poem *Orlando furioso*, the *Satire*, and the comedies. Jefferson could also read *Orlando furioso* in John Harrington's English translation published in a deluxe edition.[42]

Important to Jefferson as a political thinker was his articulate and sustained interest in Machiavelli's political oeuvre, as indicated by surviving volumes and records including Jefferson's hand-written catalogue designating the works to be donated to the Library of Congress. He purchased two volumes of Machiavelli's *Opera* in 1764,[43] though they are not known to have survived. The oldest extant edition that he held was a 1639 Latin translation of the *Prince* included in *Vindicae contra Tyrannos: sive, de principis in Populum, Populiq[ue] in Principem, legitima potestate*, a miscellany of texts on princely rule and the obligation to obey commands of a prince counter to one's religious law. The volume's margins bear notes indexing the contents and referring to other works by Machiavelli in

[42] Ludovico Ariosto, *Opere di Ariosto*, 4 vols. (Venice: Pitteri, [1741]), Sowerby, vol. 4, 436 #4311; *id.*, *Orlando Furioso in English Heroical Verse*, trans. Sir John Harrington, 3rd ed. (London: G. Miller for T. Parker, 1634), Sowerby, vol. 4, 436 #4312.
[43] Kimball, 106.

a hand that appears close to the date of publication. Sowerby, who notes Jefferson's initialling of two of the quires, documents his citing of two of the other works included.[44]

Jefferson also owned the great Ellis Farneworth English translation of Machiavelli's works published in London, Edinburgh, and Dublin in 1762, which he also initialed. A comprehensive edition enhanced by a multifaceted scholarly apparatus, it comprised political and historical writings, letters, and literary works. The latter include one of the most popular, the tale of the archdevil Belfagor who came to earth to verify if wives were the cause of so many men ending up in the nether kingdom.[45] In his Translator's Preface (Vol. 1, v-ix), Farneworth gives valuable examples of the complexity of Machiavelli's language and notes errors in earlier translations that he has corrected. Each of the two volumes is prefaced by an "Advertisement to the Reader" (Vol. 1, xiii-xvi; Vol. 2, v-viii), brought forward from the French translation by the Protestant Tetard, highlighting features of interest to prospective readers. They provide a highly articulated example of what Jacob Soll has recently discerned as the critique of abuse of power as preliminary to the Enlightment's proposal of more-egalitarian forms of govern-

---

[44] Sowerby, vol. 3, 1-2 #2324. The manuscript comments show particular interest in the Italian town of Forlì, famously contested in the Renaissance.

[45] Sowerby, vol. 3, 22 #2353; numerous letters added at the end of volume 2 (195-227 and following, unnumbered pages) have been shown by later research to be apocryphal or written over Machiavelli's signature by others; these include the purported letter to Zanobi Buondelmonte, which Farneworth had already discerned as not by Machiavelli: "Translator's Preface," vi.

ment.[46] In the first volume, the features include the study of the "wiles" used by the Medici to attain sovereignty that will enable readers to recognize and block similar strategies among the power-hungry of their time and thereby "preserve the Liberties of a free State" (xiii). Others deemed important are the instruments needed to form a strong system of laws that will prevent a government from "degenerat[ing] into insupportable Tyranny" (xiv). While praising the candor and courage with which Machiavelli, in a treatise dedicated to Pope Clement VII (Giulio de' Medici), blames the popes for the conquest of Italy through their calling in of powerful foreign allies who turned conquerors, the author also considers whether Machiavelli, an ardent participant in the Florentine Republic, could have used his writings to assist the Medici to achieve control over his city. He weighs the advantages and disadvantages of principalities and republics, and how the latter might best be structured and function. The second volume's "Advertisement" focuses on the hypocrisy of the Catholic Church in condemning the works of Machiavelli while raising to sainthood Louis IX, who cruelly persecuted the Albigensians. Among the other valuable paratextual elements are two with opposite perspectives: Abraham-Nicholas Amelot de La Houssaye's translator's preface (Vol. 1, 496-502) defending Machiavelli's text as an instrument for revealing and fighting tyranny and Voltaire's

---

[46] Jacob Soll, *Publishing* The Prince. *History, Reading, and the Birth of Political Criticism* (Ann Arbor: University of Michigan Press, 2008).

Anti-Machiavel, also known as *Examen du Prince de Machiavel*, written at the behest of the Crown Prince of Prussia, whose comments condemning *The Prince* are interleaved with its chapters [47]

Jefferson's collection of works by Machiavelli also included individual volumes indicative of his personal interests. He owned free-standing copies of the *Arte della Guerra del Machiavelli* (consistent with the prominence of war in the lives of colonial men of his generation) and of the *Poetiche del Machiavelli*, as he termed them in his hand-written catalogue. While the two volumes apparently never arrived at the Library of Congress and no more is known about them, Sowerby deduces a purchase in Paris for the *Poetiche*.[48]

Other works of Machiavelli's were selected from another edition, published in Italian in Paris and London in 1767-68. From its eight volumes, someone—likely Jefferson or another at his instruction—assembled two pairs of volumes (Sowerby notes that each was "a made up volume" whose binding is probably attributable to Jefferson). The first pair of volumes unites the *Discorsi sopra la prima deca di Tito Livio*, which originally occupied all of Volume IV and part of Volume V, with *Il Principe*, which originally occupied part of Volume III. The second pair

---

[47] The interpretation of Amelot de La Houssaye summarizes Soll, 99-102. For the latter, see Voltaire, *Anti-Machiavel*, ed. Werner Bahner and Helga Bergmann, *The Complete Works of Voltaire*, vol. 19 (Oxford: Voltaire Foundation, 1996).

[48] See Sowerby, vol. 1, 517 #1143 and vol. 4, 550 #4579.

unites other contents of Volume III — a series of letters on governmental issues and missions and the *Decennale primo* and *Decennale secondo* (presentations in poetic form of Machiavelli's insightful summary of the preceding decade's events) — with material from Volume VII. The latter texts include a second set of letters preceded by a historical preface and Machiavelli's report on his mission to Cesare Borgia (Duca Valentino). In assembling this volume, the binder accidentally inserted a quire of the second group between pages clxxv and clxxvi of the first group. The error was noted by a careful early reader, who at the bottom of clxxv penned an instruction to connect it with the remainder of the text: "turn forward 11 leaves." Of almost equal interest to the texts included are those omitted: from Volume III *La vita di Castruccio Castracani*, *Descrizzione del modo tenuto dal Duca Valentino*, *Ritratti delle cose della Francia*, *Ritratti delle cose della Magna*; from Volume V *L'arte della guerra*; from Volume VII all of the poetry. Completely neglected are the contents of the first two volumes, principally the *Istorie fiorentine* (Florentine Histories) and various paratextual elements and other texts dealing specifically with Florence and Machiavelli.

On the basis of the choices, it seems reasonable to hypothesize that Jefferson wished a copy in the original Italian of Machiavelli's most famous work, *Il Principe*, of which he may already have owned a Latin and an English translation, and also wished as many of Machiavelli's governmental reports as possible, including those of diplomatic missions to foreign powers. It seems reasonable to hypothesize further that Jefferson's purchase of the separate *Arte della guerra* and *Poetiche* is related to the omission of these texts from the selection of the 1767-68 edition, either that he did not need them from that edition because he already owned them or that, not having selected them from the 1767-68 edition, he filled in the lacunae later or from other editions. There is a further consideration of omissions from his library: while extreme caution is required in an argument from absence, it should be said that there is no evidence that Jefferson's library ever contained two sixteenth-century treatises on the republic central to the thread tracked by Pocock, the much-published works of Donato Giannotti and Gaspare Contarini that mystified and idealized in particular the Republic of Venice.[49]

Jefferson's interest in Machiavelli's commentary on Livy's work, *Discorsi sopra la prima deca di Tito Livio*, may have been generated by his own interest in Livy's work. Jefferson would eventually own two Latin editions and one Italian one of it, the last of which bears his name

[49] The claims in Giannotti's and Contarini's works, for example, that the workings of the Venetian government were known only to its patricians, that Venice had no early political trauma, that the origins of the Maggior Consiglio were unknown, and that Venice had no militia (Pocock, 280-328) were easily knowable as false. The Tiepolo conspiracy as the republic's founding trauma and the subsequent creation of the Maggior Consiglio to stabilize governance by limiting the voting population, the constant reports to and from Venice about government matters, and the Venetian creation of the peasant defensive *cernida* admired and imitated by Machiavelli were widely known to contemporaries, certainly to the Venetian patrician Contarini and to the highly-placed Giannotti.

inked on the title pages (Sowerby notes that the addition "appears to be by Jefferson, signing his name in an Italian form") and extensive underscoring.[50] Given Kevin Hayes's observation that "Because Jefferson stopped inscribing the title pages of his books before the Shadwell fire, surviving books containing title-page inscriptions in his hand must have been in his possession already,"[51] this volume appears to be from Jefferson's earliest library.

In the late fifteenth through early sixteenth centuries, Italian states suffered a transition from independence to dominance by the Holy Roman Empire resulting from the Habsburg-Valois wars for control of the peninsula. Two copies of the *Istoria d'Italia* (History of Italy), an account of the wars' events by Francesco Guicciardini, a Florentine nobleman with ties to the Medici and a more aristocratic perspective than Machiavelli, figured among the volumes ordered by Mazzei in 1774. Jefferson owned it in a 1738-1739 edition that admits it to candidacy as the second copy. Clearly designed for an expert readership, the edition includes marginal annotations, footnotes, and an index, as well as a new biography of Guicciardini and a history of the editions and the reception of his text written by Apostolo Zeno, the leading contemporary bibliographer and bibliophile of Venice. It also includes an essay by Venetian patrician Pietro Garzoni defending his republic against Guicciardini's accusation of Venetian capitulation to Maximilian after an early

---

[50] Sowerby, vol. 1, 26 #53.
[51] Hayes, 7.

defeat in the wars of Cambrai (1509-1517). Moreover, Garzoni assigns to Guicciardini's manipulations significant responsibility for Florence's acceptance of the absolute rule of the Medici Grand Dukes. In contrast, he points out, the Venetian patriciate emerged from the Italian wars with its republican government and independence intact.[52] In an interesting editorial detail, while dedicated to the Grand Duke of Tuscany, the edition was published in Venice by Giambattista Pasquali. Pasquali would later publish Goldoni's comedies, seen as so subversive of Venice's authoritarian patriciate that the playwright, fearing reprisal from the Council of Ten, urgently quit his city for Paris, where he lived and staged his works at the time of Jefferson's residence.

Intertwined both intellectually and editorially are the sixteenth-century humanist and theologian Desiderius Erasmus and Lucian of Samosata: the ancient Greek writer's questioning of excessive power in his dialogues inspired the Dutch defender of free will who translated them in his opposition to Lutheran predestination. Jefferson owned multiple editions of Lucian's works and one of Erasmus's (see below). Although Bernard Bailyn has noted Lucian's popularity in the American colonies, scholars of the history of ideas have yet to articulate his influence on colonial thinkers through his own works and through the works of other classical authors whom he influenced and

---

[52] Pietro Garzoni, "Riflessioni del N.H. s. Pietro Garzoni sopra il Guicciardini," in Francesco Guicciardini, *Istoria d'Italia*, 2 vols. (Venice: Giambattista Pasquali, 1738-39), unnumbered front matter; for Garzoni, see Giuseppe Gullino, "Garzoni, Pietro," *Dizionario Biografico degli Italiani* 52 (1999).

who were popular with colonial thinkers. His emphasis on friendship and self-governance are likely factors.

Both writer and actor, Lucian presented himself as a "seriocomic sophist who engages his audience in a playful reappraisal of the contemporary value of its celebrated cultural past." Through a blend of "pleasure and usefulness" and skillful allusions to a range of earlier writers, Lucian made appealing to a large audience his reevaluations of earlier "traditions and institutions" in the light of changed historical circumstances.[53] Part of his long-standing appeal too may be his life story, recounted in his "Dream": the modest origins requiring him to learn a profession and how, after considering the law, he apprenticed with a sculptor uncle but, inspired by a dream, chose the profession of writer and performer as more prestigious, more conducive to personal liberty, and cleaner than his uncle's sweaty work.

Interest in Lucian was rekindled in the Renaissance with the translation of his dialogues into Latin. Contemporary adaptations soon appeared. The earliest known one

---

[53] For Lucian in the colonies and Jefferson's attention to the classics, see Bernard Bailyn, *Ideological Origins of the American Revolution* (Cambridge and London: The Belknap Press of Harvard University Press, 1967) 24-25; Mullett; on Lucian, see Edward Surtz, S.J., *The Praise of Pleasure. Philosophy, Education, and Communism in More's* Utopia (Cambridge: Harvard University Press, 1957), quotation 140-41; for reception in classical period, see R. Bracht Branham, *Unruly Eloquence. Lucian and the Comedy of Traditions*, Revealing Antiquity 2 (Cambridge: Harvard University Press, 1989), quotation 7; for Lucian reception by More see also Gerard Wegemer, *Young Thomas More and the Arts of Liberty* (Cambridge: Cambridge University Press, 2011), esp. 57-69; for Lucian reception by Erasmus, see Christopher Robinson, *Lucian and His Influence in Europe* (Chapel Hill: The University of North Carolina Press, 1979), esp. 165-97; and see Eiléan Ní Chuilleanáin, "Motives of translation: More, Erasmus and Lucian," *Hermathena* 183 (Winter, 2007): 49-62.

was Matteo Maria Boiardo's play *Timone* written about 1490 for Ercole d'Este, which achieved a level of acclaim such that, according to some critics, Shakespeare modeled his *Timon of Athens* on it rather than Lucian's original.[54] Lucian's influence vastly increased with the printing of his works, first in Florence in 1496 and especially with the 1506 publication in Paris by Thomas More and Erasmus of their translations of five of his dialogues. The edition also included their responses to (largely refutations of) Lucian's *Tyrannicida*, in which he justified (some would say advocated) the killing of a tyrant's son to protect the public from the line's usurpation of power. "The book was acclaimed by scholars all over Western Europe and was reprinted eight times, in Paris, Venice, Basel, Florence, and Lyons, during More's lifetime."[55] A more recent count puts the number of editions by 1535 at fourteen.[56] As Edward Surtz noted, both More and Erasmus valued Lucian for "his unceasing war against religious imposture."[57] The Florentine edition, published by the Giuntine press in 1519 and accompanied by the first known printing in Italy of More's *Utopia*, was produced by young Florentine republicans searching for alternatives to Medici rule after the death of Lorenzo duke of Urbino. It appears to have inspired their anti-Medici plot of 1521, as Carlo Dionisotti

---

[54] Ireneo Sanesi, *La commedia*, 2 vols. (Milan: Vallardi, 1954), vol. 1, 216-17.

[55] Jasper Ridley, *The Statesman and the Fanatic. Thomas Wolsey and Thomas More* (London: Constable, 1982), 86.

[56] R. Bracht Branham, "Utopian Laughter: Lucian and Thomas More," *Moreana* 86 (1985): 23-43, 23.

[57] Surtz, *Praise*, 27-28.

observed.[58] The connection with More's *Utopia* was not casual: his character Hythloday included Lucian among his recommended authors and his very Utopians, who prized the Greek author, assassinated the ruler whom they may have considered a tyrant for his driving them to go to war.[59]

Jefferson, who demonstrated a lifelong devotion to classical Greek, owned the 1563 Basel edition of Lucian's works in the original with a flanking Latin translation, the epitome of Renaissance Lucian scholarship. It contains, as noted by Sowerby, "Manuscript marginal notes in Greek and English (including one calling attention to the missing signature) some of which may be by Jefferson."[60] Further indications that the edition was an object of study by Jefferson and his circle emerge from a comparison of it with the deluxe Amsterdam 1743 edition that he also owned. Similarly bilingual, the latter was thoroughly researched and, as the extensive scholarly apparatus indicates, based on the work of More, Erasmus (including in it his response to the *Tyrannicida*), and other scholars. As Sowerby adds, "[Thomas Frognall] Dibdin describes this edition as being not only the most beautiful but the most accurate and

---

[58] Carlo Dionisotti, "La testimonianza del Brucioli," in *Machiavellerie*, Einaudi paperbacks 113 (Turin: Einaudi, 1980) 193-226, esp. 210-13.

[59] See the complex considerations on this point by Edward Surtz, S.J., *The Praise of Wisdom. A Commentary on the Religious and Moral Problems and Backgrounds of St. Thomas More's* Utopia (Chicago: Loyola University Press, 1957) 290-91. Jefferson owned two editions of *Utopia* published before 1776: a 1555 edition in the original Latin and a 1743 English translation, both of which he initialed: Sowerby, vol. 3, 15-16 #2337 and #2338.

[60] Sowerby, vol. 5, 1 #4616; on knowledge of Greek, see e.g. the numerous passages in his *Literary Commonplace Book* and letters to John Adams.

complete that has ever been printed." The precision of the text is honored by the paucity of readerly marginal corrections, only "[s]mall marginal notes in Vol. I and II, pages 31 and 802 respectively, [that] could be by George Wythe, who bequeathed his library to Jefferson."[61] The second correction is important, however, consisting of the addition in ink of the name of a character missing from the text, together with an 'x' inked at its insertion point in the middle of the line. The correction reveals close readerly attention in that the printing conventions of the time embedded the names and speeches of characters in a running text rather than breaking the line between the conclusion of one speech and the beginning of the next.

The philologically authoritative Amsterdam edition apparently served as a source for the numerous manuscript corrections to the Basel edition, where, as Sowerby noted, Jefferson also initialed quires 'i' and 'I', 't' and 'T' "and their multiples whenever they occur." In the Basel edition there are marginal corrections to the Greek text in ink on vol. 1, 13, 114, 267, 271; the missing title of the work is inked in at the top of page 145; a note in Latin on a Greek word is inserted at the bottom of 15; and underscoring or marginal marks are made on 20, 21, 47, 100-101, 136, 285, 289, 530-31, 539, 541, 590, many passages of *Toxaris sive amicitia* 591-669, and 789. In volume 2 there are marks or underlinings on 409, 410, 411, 412, 419, 420, 425, 430; corrections to the Greek on 15, 36,

---

[61] Sowerby, vol. 5, 2 #4617.

39, 157, 160, 162, 592, 603, 611, 615, 905, 910, 912, 914, 922; and a cross-reference on 167. An attentive comparison reveals that the corrections entered into the Basel edition correspond to the compendium of the *errata corrige* of the Amsterdam edition (V-XII; 772ff *Index in scholia et varias lectiones*). Signs of readerly attention in the form of non-linguistic marginal marks are most numerous to the pages of the *Toxaris*, a work extolling friendship, and are missing from those of the *Tyrannicida*.

That the Basel edition was the 'working copy' of Lucian's texts, so to speak, seems to be indicated also by the fact that the page numbers of the works as they appear there are pencilled into the 1664 French translation of Lucian's works also owned by Jefferson, pencilling that, in Sowerby's opinion, was done by Jefferson.[62] That the page numbers were taken from the index to the Basel edition rather than from the pages themselves is demonstrated by the case of the work *Contre un Homme qui l'avoit appellé Prometée*, where the pencilled annotation gives "1.27" as in the Index, whereas the text actually begins on 24. Moreover, the index to the Basel edition bears tick marks beside the titles of works that also occur in the French translation, while on other pages marginal notations cross-reference works to their page numbers in the French translation,[63] in which the *Tyrannicida* does not appear.

---

[62] Sowerby, vol. 5, 2 #4618.

[63] See e.g. vol. 1, 164, 165, bearing the annotated numbers 39 and 40, the page numbers in the French translation on which the same work, *Prometheus seu Caucasus*, begins; see also vol. 1, 177-92 of the Basel edition, where a quire is

Jefferson's interest in Erasmus's own works is demonstrated in the acquisition of a 1693 edition of his *Colloquia* furnished with a scholarly apparatus of philological notes, an index including concepts as well as names, and a portrait of Erasmus at work in his study.[64] The Dutch scholar's incomparable knowledge of classical Greek and his defense of free will likely figured among his attractions to Jefferson.

Perhaps the most progressive work in Jefferson's library is an eighteenth-century English collection of texts on irregular conjugal practices, including a translation of Bernardino Ochino's mid-sixteenth-century treatise on polygamy.[65] As detailed in a lengthy biographical essay prefacing the translation, Ochino was a prominent preacher and leader of the Capuchin order. He became involved in the Italian evangelical reform movement to the point that, despite advancing years, he fled to Switzerland out of fear of ecclesiastical prosecution. However, his functionalist approach to religious issues led him to reject various Protestant doctrines there as well, especially predestination. He wrote dialogues on numerous religious issues to bring them to a larger public. The dialogue on polygamy advanc-

---

missing: the reference to it appears both there and in the French translation in vol. 1, 53, where the missing section occurs in the translation.

[64] Erasmus, *Colloquia*, cum notis selectis Variorum. Addito Indice novo. Accurante Corn. Schrevelio. Amsterdami, Ex Typographia Blaviana, MDCXCIII; Sowerby, vol. 5, 3-4 #4622.

[65] *The Cases of Polygamy, Adultery, Concubinage, Divorce, etc. Seriously and Learnedly Discussed. Being a Compleat Collection of all the Remarkable Tryals and Tracts which have been Written on those Important Subjects By the most Eminent Hands.* London: Printed for T. Payne, in Pater-Noster Row; J. Chrichley, at Charing-Cross; and W. Shropshire, in New-Bond Street, 1732; Sowerby, vol. 2, 51 #1358.

es reasons for and against multiple spouses for both wom-
en and men, a proposal made decades earlier by Paduan
comic playwright Angelo Beolco (Il Ruzante), of which
Ochino is likely to have known through his connections to
Venice and Verona.[66] While Ochino's dialogue opens by
proposing polygamy to resolve the dilemma of a man with
a sickly and sterile wife wishing to comply with Biblical instructions to have many children, it closes with a radical
notion. To the query of interlocutor A about what to do if
God does not give him the gift of removing his desire for
multiple wives, the authoritative interlocutor B responds:
"If you then do that to which God shall incline you, so that
you are sure that you are led by Divine Instigation, you
shall not err. For it can be no Error to obey God" (65).
Thus Ochino fuses personal wishes, including those counter to established Christian codes of behavior, with divine
will, a step in the Western progression in the identity of the
central authorizer from God to the "ordinary man" observed by Michel de Certeau.[67]

The final monument of late Renaissance Italian literature, Torquato Tasso's religious epic *Gerusalemme libera-*

[66] Angelo Beolco (Il Ruzante), *La prima oratione*, ed. and trans. Linda L. Carroll, MHRA Critical Texts Vol. 16 (London: Modern Humanities Research
Association, 2009) 98-101; I am grateful to the American Philosophical Society
for a grant to read the manuscripts of Beolco works on which this edition is
based. Both Beolco and Ochino proposed polygamy, multiple spouses for both
partners; other reformers proposed polygyny, multiple wives only: see Linda L.
Carroll, "A Nontheistic Paradise in Renaissance Padua," *Sixteenth Century
Journal* 24 (1993): 881-98, 884.
[67] Michel de Certeau, *The Practice of Everyday Life*, trans. Steven F. Rendall
(Berkeley and Los Angeles: University of California Press, 1984) 4.

ta, was owned by Jefferson in three editions: two deluxe illustrated editions in Italian of 1745 and 1763 and John Hoole's English translation of 1764.[68] Jefferson's appreciation of the text, which may have been one of the first books he owned, is expressed in his inclusion of it, the sole work of Italian literature, in the list of essential books that he recommended to his friend Robert Skipwith in 1771 and of his play on a quotation from a speech of Clorinda's in a letter to the Count de Volney.[69]

---

[68] Torquato Tasso, *La Gerusalemme Liberata di Torquato Tasso con le Figure di Giambatista Piazzetta alla sacra rea Maestà Maria Teresa d'Austria Regina d'Ungheria, e di Boemia, ec.* In Venezia, MDCCXLV. Stampata da Giambatista Albrizzi q. Girol. Con Privilegio dell'Eccellentissimo Senato (Sowerby, vol. 4, 425 #4290); Torquato Tasso, *La Gierusalemme Liberata di Torquato Tasso: con le Figure di Sebastiano Clerc. In Due Volumi. In Glasgua: della Stampa di Roberto ed Andrea Foulis, e si vendeno Appresso Loro, e Giovanni Balfour in Edinburgo, MDCCLXIII* (Sowerby, vol. 4, 425-26 #4291); Torquato Tasso, *Jerusalem Delivered; an Heroic Poem: translated from the Italian of Torquato Tasso, by John Hoole. The Second Edition. London: Printed for R. and J. Dodsley, P. Vaillant, T. Davies, J. Newbery and Z. Stuart*, MDCCLXIV (Sowerby, vol. 4, 426 #4292).
[69] Jefferson, *Papers*, ed. Boyd, Vol. 1 *1760-1776*, 78; Hayes, 433-34; Wilson, 164-65.

Seventeenth-Century Italian Philosophy and Science

The early seventeenth century's crucial episode in the freeing of the state from church controls, the papal interdict on the Venetian Republic (1606-1607), is well represented in Jefferson's library in works by and concerning the learned Servite friar Paolo Sarpi. By the early seventeenth century, increased public involvement in religious issues and efforts by the Catholic Church to reinforce its authority in Italy had intensified conflict between Venice and the papacy. The chief precipitating issue, culminating a century of strife that had begun with the wars of the League of Cambrai, was Venice's assertion of control in its territorial state of the appointment of bishops, of the establishment of religious entities, and of the rights over real properties claimed by ecclesiastical entities. When the pope issued a brief rejecting the assertion, the Venetian government called upon Paolo Sarpi for advice in the matter. The first question to be addressed was Venice's possible future appeal to a council of cardinals, a burning issue because in the early fifteenth century such a council had resolved the three rival claims to the papacy by declaring its authority as higher than the pope's because of its authority to elect the pope. Among the sources Sarpi consulted were those conciliarists, whose strategies were described in Francesco Griselini's meticulous biography of the Servite that Jefferson owned and initialled, including the page with the history of the London printing of

Sarpi's history of the Council of Trent (see below).[70]

For the conciliarists, among whom Cardinal Francesco Zabarella of Padua was a leading figure, the pope "was not an absolute monarch but in some sense a constitutional ruler" to whom the community had delegated its authority of self-rule while retaining "whatever residual power was necessary to prevent its own subversion or destruction ... via its representatives assembled in a general council ... in certain critical cases even against the wishes of the pope ... and even depose the pope," to quote Francis Oakley.[71] Again one is reminded of the Declaration: "That to secure these rights, Governments are instituted among Men, deriving their just powers from the consent of the governed, — That whenever any Form of Government becomes destructive of these ends, it is the Right of the People to alter or to abolish it, and to institute new Government...". According to conciliarists, the Church lacked worldly powers

---

[70] Francesco Griselini, *Memorie anedote spettanti alla Vita ed agli studj del sommo Filosofo e Giureconsulto F. Paolo Sarpi Servita raccolte ed ordinate da Francesco Griselini Veneziano, della celebre Accademia dell'Istituto delle Scienze di Bologna,* Edizione Seconda, Corretta, e considerabilmente accresciuta. In Losana, Apresso Giovanni Nestenus e Comp. MDCCLX, 88-96; Sowerby, vol. 1, 292 #617, giving Jefferson's title for it in his catalogue ("Vita del Padre Paolo del Griselini") and noting "Initialed by Jefferson at sigs. I and T." The further detail could be added that on 289, which contains the history of the printing in London, Jefferson added his 'J' in ink to the pre-existing quire mark 'T', which he did not do on the other pages of the quire also bearing the 'T'. Of modern scholarship on the Interdict, see William J. Bouwsma, *Venice and the Defense of Republican Liberty* (Berkeley and Los Angeles: University of California Press, 1968), notes 74 and 79 below.

[71] Francis Oakley, "The 'New Conciliarism' and Its Implications: A Problem in History and Hermeneutics," *Journal of Ecumenical Studies* 8 (1971): 815-40, 818-19; see also Brian Tierney, "Franciscus Zabarella," Chapter IV in *Foundations of Conciliar Theory* (Cambridge: Cambridge University Press, 1955) 220-37.

for several reasons: juridical powers belonged to the civil state; in its original state, Church governance was democratic, with the hierarchy created only later and by humans; the pope, as merely the bishop of Rome among other bishops, had only a morally central role in the church that did not confer coercive authority over the behavior of others; the authority of the council of cardinals was superior to that of the pope.[72] Conciliarism was revived in the sixteenth century by those attempting to limit the reach of its autocratic popes.[73] Sarpi advised the Venetian government that he concurred with the conciliarists' views on the superior authority of the council and subsequently wrote a response to Rome and a number of other works on the issues involved.[74]

These included a detailed *Historia del Concilio tridentino* (History of the Council of Trent) casting the previous century of papal activities as directed toward political control of Europe,[75] against which Sarpi defended the independence of civic governments from ecclesiastical authority. Considered too dangerous to be published in Italy, the treatise was smuggled out and published in Eng-

---

[72] Early Church history was a subject that fascinated Jefferson as expressed in his letters to John Adams of October 13, 1813 and of August 15, 1820.

[73] Francis Oakley, "Conciliarism at the Fifth Lateran Council?" *Church History* 41 (1972): 452-63.

[74] See Corrado Vivanti, "Introduzione," in Paolo Sarpi, *Istoria del Concilio Tridentino*, 2 vols (Turin: Giulio Einaudi, 1974) vol. 1, XXIX-XCII and see also "Cronologia per la *Istoria del Concilio Tridentino* (1500-64) e per la vita di Paolo Sarpi (1552-1623)," XCIX-CLX, esp. CXLII-CXLVI; David Wootton, *Paolo Sarpi* (Cambridge: Cambridge University Press, 1983) 45-68.

[75] See especially Sarpi, *Istoria*, vol. 2, 1188-99 "Capitolo della riforma de' principi sopra le immunità ecclesiastiche."

land under the anagrammatic pseudonym Pietro Soave Polano.[76] In no small part because it was written by a Catholic friar, James I welcomed it as bolstering both his civil authority and the Protestant cause.[77]

Jefferson owned Sarpi's treatise in an Italian edition that was bound for him, which he initialled and in which he possibly entered a correction; he also owned an English translation that he initialled. On the title page of the latter, in a rare departure from his usual restraint in annotating books, he wrote a note accepting the view expressed in Collier's dictionary that Sarpi had written his treatise in response to an anti-Venetian work written in 1607, the *Squitinio [Scrutinio] della liberta Veneta*, which Jefferson also owned[78]: "The Venetians persuading F. Paul to write an answer to a book lately published, called 'Scrutinio della libertà Veneta' he told them he had an answer ready, and delivered to them his History of the Council of Trent which Marcus Antonius de Dominis took upon him to publish, & got it printed in London under the name of Pietro Soave Polano, which is the Anagram of Paolo Sarpi Veneto. v. Collier's dict. voce Sarpi."[79] Note Jefferson's use of the Latin-derived Italian

---

[76] Gaetano Cozzi, "Fra Paolo Sarpi, l'anglicanesimo e la *Historia del Concilio Tridentino,*" *Rivista storica italiana* 68 (1956): 559-619; *id., Paolo Sarpi tra Venezia e l'Europa* (Turin: Einaudi, 1978).

[77] See Nicla Riverso, "Paolo Sarpi: The Hunted Friar and his Popularity in England," in *Speaking Truth to Power from Medieval to Modern Italy,* ed. Jo Ann Cavallo and Carlo Lottieri, *Annali d'Italianistica* 34 (2016): 297-318.

[78] Sowerby, vol. 3, 43 #2412, apparently unrecognized by her under the variant titles *Examen* and *Squitinio.*

[79] Paolo Sarpi, *Historia del Concilio tridentino di Pietro Soave Polano. Quarta Editione, riveduta e corretta dall'autore.* In Geneva, Appresso Pietro Chouët. MDCLX; Sowerby, vol. 1, 291 #615, where she notes that it was bound for

term *voce* ('entry in a reference work'). Jefferson thus gives evidence of his awareness of the effects of the restraint of publishing freedom, which as a bibliophile he is likely to have noted in the publication of many of his Italian volumes outside of Italy. Given Hayes's observation that Jefferson refrained from such annotations on title pages after the Shadwell fire and Jefferson's 1769 commission to Matthew Maury to purchase books for him in England, it is possible that the English edition of Sarpi's works figured among Jefferson's earliest books.[80] The union of unusual erudition and unusual commitment to self-governance in such a choice is characteristic of his twin lifelong passions.[81]

In his argumentation, Sarpi defended the authority of

Jefferson, who initialled it and possibly entered a correction; Paolo Sarpi, *The Historie of the Covncel of Trent. Conteining eight Bookes....Second Edition, ...* London: Printed by Bonham Norton and John Bill, MDCXXIX; Sowerby, vol. 1, 291-92 #616, where she notes that it was initialled by Jefferson and transcribes the note, her lack of reference to the *Scrutinio* under the variant *Squitinio* in the *Examin de la liberté originaire de Venice* that Jefferson also owned (see below) apparently indicating that she did not realize that it was the text to which Jefferson referred. Louis Moréri and Jeremy Collier, *The great historical, geographical, genealogical and poetical dictionary; being a curious miscellany of sacred and prophane history. ... Collected from the best historians, chronologers, and lexicographers; ... especially out of Lewis Morery, ... The second edition revis'd, corrected and enlarg'd to the year 1688; by Jer. Collier, A. M.,* Vol. 2, Printed for Henry Rhodes; Thomas Newborough; the assigns of L. Meredith; and Elizabeth Harris, 1701, *s.v.* and for Jefferson's 1721 edition, see Sowerby, vol. 1, 67-68 #145. This was the accepted account and may have been based on Griselini (249ff, 267), according to whom Sarpi began his history as a response to the *Scrutinio* but was distracted from it by more serious matters. According to current research, Sarpi worked on the *Historia* from about 1610 to 1618. On knowledge of Sarpi in Jefferson's day, see also John D. Bessler, *The Celebrated Marquis. An Italian Noble and the Making of the Modern World* (Durham, NC: Carolina Academic Press, 2018), 225.

[80] Jefferson, *Memorandum Books*, vol. 1, 143.

[81] See Wilson, "Jefferson's Library," 162.

civil government as both delegated to it by the populace it governed and conferred directly by God, the former rendering it superior to ecclesiastical authority. The formulation, in which human delegation ranked above divine delegation, daringly advanced the 'ascending' thesis over the traditional sole 'descending' thesis of ecclesiastical authority as superior because conferred by God. Sarpi's views clearly derive from the theory formulated in the fourteenth century by Marsilius of Padua and William of Ockham of the right of the human community to self-government, views developed by the medieval legal experts and conciliarists discussed above and revived in the sixteenth century in the wake of the Lutheran reform and the increasing control of the Catholic Church by its hierarchy.[82] An important touchstone was Marsilius's *Defensor pacis*, first published in Latin in Basel in 1522 and subsequently in English in 1535, in German in 1545, and again in Latin in Germany in 1592 and 1599.[83] As noted by Gregorio Piaia, Sarpi and others defending Venice used many arguments similar to those of Marsilius and structured them similarly. Although they did not acknowledge using Marsilius as an authority, likely because of ecclesiastical opprobrium for him, their opponents accused them of doing so. As Piaia notes, with Marsilius's text so readily available, it is likely that Sarpi knew of it and it is known that he read Gallican theorists who drew on it.

---

[82] Gregorio Piaia, *Marsilio da Padova nella Riforma e nella Controriforma. Fortuna ed interpretazione* (Padua: Antenore, 1977) 395-403; Tierney, *Idea*, 185.

[83] Piaia, 437.

Sarpi, who was primarily a scientist (the editor's preface to the Griselini biography praises his discoveries in anatomy and anticipation of both Locke on certain issues of metaphysics and many discoveries of the most advanced thinkers of the eighteenth century [xviii]), met Galileo Galilei in Padua in 1589. They developed a friendly professional relationship after 1592, when Galileo was named a professor at the University of Padua, a leading institution in the scientific disciplines. Galileo believed that Sarpi, who reconciled the movements of the heavenly bodies into a single system, was the most expert mathematician in Europe. He enlisted him in his improvements to the telescope and called on him as an expert witness to his invention of the *compasso geometrico e militare* (geometric and military compass; see below). The two maintained an active correspondence, with Galileo mentioning Sarpi numerous times in his works, which Jefferson owned.[84]

Jefferson's multi-volume Paduan edition of Galileo's works, which includes a lengthy historical preface, recorded his inventions, discoveries, and defense of both. The best-known of the inventions, an improved telescope, attracted the support of Venice, which was seeking a navigational aid to return it to primacy in maritime commerce and which

---

[84] Vivanti, "Cronologia," CXXXV-CLII; David Wootton, *Galileo: Watcher of the Skies* (New Haven: Yale University Press, 2010) 3-5, 45, 57, 61-64, 80, 83, 89, 91, 126, 143, 149, 175, 249-50; Galileo Galilei, *Opere di Galileo Galilei divise in quattro tomi, In questa nuova Edizione accresciute di molte cose inedite ...* In Padova, MDCCXLIV, Nella Stamperia del Seminario. Appresso Gio: Manfrè, Con licenza de' superiori e privilegio, Sowerby, vol. 4, 67 #3786; references to Sarpi: vol. 1, 144-45, 151, 155-62 (155 his excellence as a mathematician); vol. 2, 558-60.

rewarded Galileo with a permanent chair at the University of Padua. However, both the academic and the ecclesiastical establishments, seeing their formerly unassailable positions undermined by Galileo's discoveries, required him to defend them. In a letter of 1612 included in the edition, Galileo couched his assertion of his discoveries' veracity in a citation of Beolco/Ruzante's emphasis on "un bon snaturale" (a good extranatural). He followed that with several lines in Ruzantine peasant dialect touting the superiority of observation over university book learning.[85]

A possible reference by Jefferson (see below) calls for a closer examination of Galileo's attachment to Ruzante. Galileo recited Ruzante's texts, and collected them and texts by other dialect writers, with whom he corresponded. He was an intimate of Giacomo Alvise Cornaro, the grandson of Ruzante's patron Alvise Cornaro, giving him some of his works in 1601. It was in Cornaro's home in 1603 that he showed his military compass to the Milanese Baldassare Capra, who subsequently copied it. Cornaro testified to the episode in 1607 as part of Galileo's defense of his invention of the compass and his theoretical explanation of a 'new star' (actually a conjunction of Jupiter, Saturn, and Mars) that had appeared in 1604, which was at odds with the theories prevailing among the professors of the Univer-

[85] Galileo, *Opere*, vol. 2, 542; cfr. Angelo Beolco (Ruzante), *Betia*, in *Teatro*, ed. Ludovico Zorzi (Turin: Einaudi, 1967) 155; Emilio Lovarini, "Galileo interprete del Ruzzante," in *Studi sul Ruzzante e sulla letteratura pavana*, ed. Gianfranco Folena (Padua: Antenore, 1965) 377-92; id., "Galileo scrittore pavano?," in *Studi*, 391-410.

sity of Padua.[86] A literary defense of Galileo's explanation of the new star was published in Padua in 1605. Written in Ruzante's country Paduan, it is a dialogue between two peasants making it plain that even the unlettered see the finding's veracity because they observe nature without bias. The dialogue is associated with Galileo and his student Girolamo Spinelli, although there is scholarly disagreement about their exact roles and the participation of additional followers of Galileo.[87] The authors clearly took pleasure in satyrizing the kind of academic experts who rejected Galileo's observations of celestial nature as they had Ruzante's observations of human nature and doing so with Ruzante's common-sense peasants and words. The episode and text raise the question of whether or not this aspect of Galileo's work informs Jefferson's affirmation, "'State a moral case to a ploughman and a professor. The former will decide it as well and often better than the latter because he has not been led astray by artificial rules'."[88]

---

[86] Galileo, "Difesa di Galileo Galilei, Nobile Fiorentino, Lettore delle Matematiche nello Studio di Padova, Contro alle Calunnie ed imposture di Baldassar Capra Milanese," in *Opere*, vol. 1, 134-88, esp. 141-42, 146-47, 152-53, 171-72.

[87] See Stillman Drake, ed., *Galileo Against the Philosophers in His* Dialogue of Cecco di Ronchitti *(1605) and* Considerations of Alimberto Mauri *(1606) in English Translations* (Los Angeles: Zeitlin and Ver Brugge, 1976); Wootton, *Galileo*, 88 and note 2 for various views; in addition to those cited, consult Lovarini, "Galileo interprete" and "Galileo scrittore."

[88] Jefferson, *Papers*, ed. Boyd, vol. 12, 15 letter to Peter Carr from Paris dated August 10, 1787, quoted in Garry Wills, *Inventing America. Jefferson's Declaration of Independence* (Garden City, NY: Doubleday, 1978), 203. In one of his works available in various Renaissance published editions, the *Seconda oratione* (Second Oration), Ruzante proposed that peasants have a law favoring them just as the city people do.

*Venice as a Model of Republican Freedom
and Government*

As the sole exemplar of the Italian medieval republics
to survive into the eighteenth century, the Venetian Republic provided a potential model to American colonials look-
ing to establish a new state. Jefferson's library included
numerous works providing in-the-round perspectives on
both the Republic's accomplishments and its defects. It is
of note that at all evidence Jefferson did not own the treatises mystifying Venice by Donato Giannotti and Gaspare
Contarini, which corresponds with his preference for real-
ism and his criticism of Venice's limiting of governance
roles to the aristocracy. The earliest of the texts that he
owned was mentioned above: *Examen de la Liberté originaire de Venise. Traduit de l'Italien. Avec une harangue de
Louis Hélian contre les Venetiens, traduit du Latin*, probably printed in 1678. An early example of the approach described by Jacob Soll, it unites two treatises disputing Venice's claims to be a beacon of freedom in its founding circumstances free of the empire, its freedom from ecclesiastical authority, and its governing practices based on elective
offices open to a large patriciate. The first, whose title in
this printing substituted *Examen* for *Squitinio* or *Scrutinio*,
was the anti-Venetian treatise written at the time of the
1606-1607 Interdict, which was attributed to Marcus Velserus (Welser) and Alfonso de la Cueva, Marquis de Ded-
mar, and first published in Mirandola in 1612. Jefferson's
familiarity with the text is demonstrated in his note to the

title page of the English edition of Sarpi's works quoted above, in which he cited the *Squitinio*, on the basis of authoritative but erroneous sources, as the text prompting Sarpi's writing of his *Historia del Concilio tridentino*.[89]

In addition to its disparagement of the Republic's claims to liberty, the *Squitinio* condemned the Republic's failure to defend its mainland state during the wars of the League of Cambrai. It characterized Venice's reaction to the crushing 1509 defeat at Agnadello as cowardly in its abandonment of the state and its sending of an ambassador to Maximilian to accept his protection as liege lord of the mainland state if he would ally with them against France. Even a century later when the *Squitinio* gave it voice, the reaction of the French was one of infuriated betrayal because of their expectation of claiming their portion of the state earlier agreed upon in the formation of the League of Cambrai and their important role in Venice's defeat. The text published with the *Squitinio* in the 1678 volume was the speech that the French ambassador Louis Hélian had delivered to the Diet of Augsburg in 1510. It reveals how quickly and completely alliances mutated in the early sixteenth century. In the year's interval, the architect of the League of Cambrai, Pope Julius II, fearing a strong France with overweening territorial ambitions in the Italian peninsula, had offered Venice an alliance. Venice accepted. Hélian's speech expressed

---

[89] See note 74 above: Sarpi wrote other texts defending Venice at the time of the Interdict and the *Historia* later.

France's response, an overture to the emperor Maximilian to form a counter alliance. The French ambassador promises Maximilian that together they can defeat the crafty Venetians, who aim to control the entire peninsula and who, because of their weakened state, are even prepared to align with the Turk against Christians.[90] American revolutionaries faced similar problems, and Jefferson feared that the attractions of aristocracy and even monarchy would lead them to betray the principles of self-government that he worked so hard to inculcate.

Another volume in Jefferson's library could have shaped Jefferson's understanding of Sarpi and of Venice. Published in 1760, it was erroneously attributed to the Servite friar: *Memoria inedita presentata al Senato Veneto dal celebre Fra Paolo Sarpi Intorno al modo da tenersi dalla Repubblica per il buono e durevol governo del suo Stato* (Unpublished Memoir Presented to the Venetian Senate by the Acclaimed Friar Paolo Sarpi On the Way

---

[90] *Examen de la Liberté originaire de Venise. Traduit de l'Italien. Avec une harangue de Louis Hélian contre les Venetiens, traduit du Latin.* Ratisbonne[?]: Jean Aubri, 1678, esp. 201-203; Sowerby, vol. 3, 43 #2412, where she gives the full title of the harangue as *Harangue de Louis Hélian Ambassadeur de France, prononcée en présence de l'Empereur Maximilien, des electeurs, des princes, des prélats, & des députés des villes de l'Empire, l'an 1510* and notes that the only edition in the catalogue of the Bibliothèque Nationale that fully corresponds to the details of Jefferson's is the Ratisbonne edition of 1678. She notes further that the first part "is a translation of *Squitinio della liberta Veneta*, Mirandola, 1612" that some have attributed to Marcus Velserus (Welser) and by others to Alfonso de la Cueva and that it was translated into French by Abraham-Nicholas Amelot de La Houssaye. On the *Squitinio* see also Griselini, 249ff, 267, 356. On the situation of Venice in 1510, see Kenneth M. Setton, *The Sixteenth Century to the Reign of Julius III*, vol. 3 of *The Papacy and the Levant (1204-1571)*, Memoirs of the American Philosophical Society, vol. 161 (Philadelphia: The American Philosophical Society, 1984) 76-90.

in Which the Republic Conducts itself for the Good and Lasting Governing of Its State).[91] Claimed by its author to have been ordered by the Doge and Inquisitors, a claim undermined by its publication "In Colonia" (Cologne? but probably Livorno, a false location to avoid the censor), the *Memoria* sets forth ways of governing that will help Venice's government endure. It praises the imposing of taxes (*gravezze*) on both nobles and their subjects. Advising officials to apply justice even-handedly to avoid the impression that the rich are favored, it prescribes both punishments of patricians for crimes to show that they are not exempt and limitations on those punishments to safeguard patrician authority. It promises officials that if they follow this advice, they will construct "a strong foundation for the state" (*un gran fondamento dello stato*) because when subjects believe that the justice system will take their side, they will put up with a great deal (13-14). Nobles are also advised to avoid dominating public offices and using them to force citizens to perform tasks. These measures will avoid a "Vespro Siciliano" (25), a reference to the thirteenth-century popular uprising in Sicily overthrowing autocratic French rule. The treatise's air of near-desperation reminds the modern reader that the Republic had less than fifty years remaining.

Jefferson acquired a fact-based, balanced, and insightful account of historical and current Venice in a lengthy work

---

[91] In Colonia [i.e. Livorno]: presso Pietro Mortier, 1760; Sowerby, vol. 3, 62 #2466.

of the late seventeenth century by a French diplomat.[92] Alexandre Toussaint Limojon de St. Didier, who had served as an assistant to the French ambassador to the Venetian Republic from 1672 to 1674, wrote *La ville et la république de Venise* to redress the erroneous depiction of Venice in other works. He praises Venice's great homes and the active commerce of products from the entire Po Valley and the sea, as well as the good treatment that foreign merchants receive in Venice. He attributes the endurance of the state to a moderated openness and a broad application of justice. In particular, he notes that the basis for stability was provided by the closing of the patriciate in 1289 together with both chastisement and appeasement of those who were excluded (127-28). He describes the structure of the Venetian government as harvesting the advantages of the three basic forms by including an element of monarchy through the doge, of aristocracy through the Senate, and of democracy through the Maggior Consiglio (Great Council) to which all patricians belong. He also describes the election of parish priests by the parishioners, which contributes to the priests' care of their flocks and transparency about their virtues and defects. Limojon dedicates considerable space to the limitations that the Republic places on Catholic institutions, especially the Inquisition and the Jesuits (181-88), and the liberality with which it treats foreigners of other religious tradi-

---

[92] Alexandre Toussaint Limojon de St. Didier, *La ville et la république de Venise*. A Paris: chez Guillaume de Luyne, MDCLXXX. Avec Privilege du Roi. Sowerby, vol. 3, 42 #2410, where she notes its initialling by Jefferson but attributes other marks on the book to others.

tions (Greek Orthodox, Lutherans, Huguenots, and especially Jews because of their financial capacity), who are
placed under civil rather than ecclesiastical jurisdiction. At
the University of Padua, which served as Venice's state university, foreign students are protected from the ecclesiastical
requirement of a profession of Catholic faith as a prerequi-
site for the degree by the conferring of degrees on all without distinction by religion in a specially designated room
(190-93). Jefferson's commitment to religious tolerance may
have made Venice's tolerance particularly appealing to
him,[93] although his opposition to an aristocratic class[94] and to
colonies made its patrician caste and mainland and maritime empires uncongenial to him.

Limojon describes each organ of the Venetian government, its tasks, and the typical profile of those elected to
it. He notes that the Senate (Pregadi) holds authority in
certain critical matters: declaring war, leagues, and alliances;
electing the generals who command the army and the ad-
mirals who command the fleet and their officers; naming
ambassadors; electing the bodies that comprise the Colle-
gio that serves as the Senate's executive committee; examin-
ing and voting on measures proposed by the Savi (Senate
committees on specific issues such as trade). The Venetian
practice of excluding those whose close relatives are eccle-
siastics from decisions concerning the Catholic Church is
noted. Here one is reminded of the third linchpin of the

---

[93] Kimball, 124-29, 215, 224-25.
[94] Kimball, 227-28.

Declaration: "laying its foundation on such principles and organizing its powers in such form, as to them shall seem most likely to effect their Safety and Happiness."

Included as well in Limojon's account is a description of the role of opera and comedy in Venetian life, whose importance is confirmed by recent research.[95] Somewhat obscured by his reputation for austerity, Jefferson's passion for theater manifested itself especially in his youthful days and during his time in Europe. While in Paris, he frequented the French and the Italian comic theaters where he saw a French adaptation of *La buona figliuola* by Carlo Goldoni, who had fled Venice for Paris to avoid the reported wrath of the Council of Ten. In his correspondence with Maria Cosway, Jefferson likened himself in reading her notes to the character Harlequin of *Les Deux Billets*, which he had seen with her.[96] Traveling in northern Italy in the spring of 1787, he purchased tickets to the theater in all the cities that had them.[97]

Cesare Beccaria's ground-breaking 1764 *Dei delitti e delle pene* (*On Crimes and Punishments*) likely entered Jefferson's library along with Montesquieu's *Ésprit des lois* in late 1769, and he immediately took extensive notes

[95] Ellen Rosand, *Opera in Seventeenth-Century Venice: The Creation of a Genre* (Berkeley and London: University of California Press, 1991); Wendy Heller, *Emblems of Eloquence. Opera and Women's Voices in Seventeenth-Century Venice* (Berkeley and London: University of California Press, 2003); Edward Muir, *Culture Wars of the Late Renaissance: Skeptics, Libertines, and Opera* (Cambridge: Harvard University Press, 2007).
[96] Hayes, 334-39.
[97] Jefferson, *Memorandum Books*, vol. 1, 73-79, 141, 142, 203-205, 210-11, 254-63, 561, 581, 608, 629 n. 28 for identification of play, 635, 638, 662-63.

from it in Italian.[98] He later acquired an English translation of it, and also owned Voltaire's 1766 commentary.[99]
John D. Bessler has chronicled the immediate and im-
mense success of Beccaria's work in both Europe and
America.[100] Its popularity, its publication in English in
London in 1767, and Mazzei's enthusiastic promotion of
it provided Jefferson with numerous opportunities to
learn of the influence of its proposals, which centered on
a strictly limited set of punishments never in excess of the
crime and on their even-handed application to all. Garry
Wills affirms that Beccaria's work was "a special favorite
of Jefferson," which he utilized in his revision of the laws
of Virginia and in his drafting of the 1774 "A Summary
View of the Rights of British America." Jefferson recommended it in his later correspondence, especially the substitution of the death penalty with useful public works.[101]

In his commentary on Beccaria's work, Voltaire expounds on the injustice of the death penalty in many cas-

---

[98] Kimball, 210-11, 224-25, 244-45; for the excerpts that he copied into his commonplace book, see Thomas Jefferson, "1762-1767, Legal Commonplace Book," Library of Congress, The Thomas Jefferson Papers at the Library of Congress, Manuscript Division, Series 5, Commonplace Books, Microfilm Reel 059, http://hdl.loc.gov/loc.mss/mtj.mtjbib026466, images 257-72, excerpts 806-31.

[99] Cesare Beccaria, *An Essay on crimes & punishments*, translated from the Italian. With a commentary, attributed to M. de Voltaire. Translated from the French...New York: published by Stephen Gould, 1809; Sowerby, vol. 3, 21 #2349, where she notes Jefferson's citing of it in his autobiography and letter; Voltaire, *Commentaire sur le livre des délits et des peines, par un avocat de Province*. Without name of place or printer but Geneva, 1766; Sowerby, vol. 3, 21 #2350.

[100] See most recently Bessler; note, however, that Elisabetta Caminer Turra was Venetian not Florentine and an important progressive journalist (74).

[101] Wills, 42-43.

es, which he attributes to religious fanaticism and to excessive severity in dealing with acts of desperation resulting from inadequate social supports. He opens the book with the example of the execution of a young woman whose child had died because, seduced and ashamed, she had abandoned it. He expresses the view that if charitable services had been available to care for the child or if the family had kept the matter to itself, both the child and the mother would have lived. He continues with further similar examples and examples of religious fanatics who cause dissenters to be burned alive and who plot even the execution of heads of state, such as the Jesuits did against King Charles of England. He also addresses the issue's practical side, noting that criminals are more valuable to the state alive than dead when their punishment is labor, which produces public works and makes them honest (52-56). Voltaire views excessive punishments as discouraging convictions because they generate pity (108-109), and sees their application to both small and large crimes as encouraging large crimes (90-91). At the bottom of 118 of Jefferson's copy is a note in English approving of works as a substitute for the death penalty and a note in French praising Jefferson for contemplating making such changes, envisioning that they will put an end to revolts against the law. According to Sowerby, they were not by Jefferson.

Pietro Verri, a close friend of Beccaria's who is believed to have been an important inspiration of the volume, was also present in Jefferson's library in a 1771 Italian edition of his work on political economy, in which he encouraged the free development of local industry and the reduction of regulations, praised banks and their mechanisms of payment, and considered various norms of taxation.[102] The objections to British limitations on American commerce to which Jefferson gave voice in "A Summary View" are similar to those of Verri, who shared doubts about the value of overseas colonies.[103]

Jefferson owned several works by his friend Filippo Mazzei. Of special interest is a short, bi-lingual tract considering an episode apparently witnessed by Mazzei in England in which a young woman falsely accused of murder by a public official, having received the support of her religious community, succeeded in turning public opinion against the official who, when he fled, was stopped by a crowd, turned over to the courts, and prosecuted. The author praises the English for their open-minded receptiveness to the facts unaffected by prejudice toward the young woman's much lower social status, the temperate willingness of the populace to apprehend a guilty party even when of the upper class but to refrain from punishing him and instead trusting the justice system, and the impartiality of the justice system in prosecuting him.[104] Mazzei wrote an

---

[102] Pietro Verri, *Meditazioni sulla economia politica*, Genova, MDCCLXXI. Presso Ivone Gravier sotto la Loggia di Banchi. Nella Stamperia di Adamo Scionico Sulla Piazza di L. Lorenzo, Con licenza de' Sup.; Sowerby, vol. 3, 443 #3556, where she notes that it was initialled by Jefferson.

[103] See *inter alia* Verri, 31, 39-43, 46-47, 101-102, 111.

[104] [Filippo Mazzei], *A Letter on the behaviour of the populace on a late occasion, in the procedure against a noble lord. Lettera Intorno al Comportamento Del Popolo Inglese In un fatto seguito ultimamente Contro un signore.* The

account of the American situation, *Recherches historiques et Politiques sur les É U de l'Amérique Septentrionale*, which benefitted from Jefferson's information, and a copy of it resided in Jefferson's library.[105] In it, Mazzei expounds on the importance of equality of the law and of governance roles for all. How radical Mazzei was in his proposals is evident in his defense of the equal rights of women including to hold office.

Finally, their early publication dates perhaps reflecting his youthful interest in literature and theater,[106] Jefferson included in his library a pastoral work translated by Gasparo Gozzi and a 9-volume collection of Italian theatrical pieces staged in France.[107] While his wife's library probably contributed an English translation of Luigi Riccoboni's history of Italian theater and a novellistic rendition in Italian of the *Vita di San Giosafato* (Life of St.

Second Edition. London: Printed by W. Bingle, opposite Durham-Yard in the Strand. MDCCLXVIII; Sowerby, vol. 5, 137 #2753, where she notes that Jefferson wrote 'Philip Mazzei' on the half title and that it is bound together with five other pamphlets by different authors; their publication dates are all in the 1760s.

[105] Philip Mazzei, *Recherches historiques et Politiques sur les É U de l'Amérique Septentrionale ...* Première [-Quatrième] partie. A. Colle, et se trouve à Paris: chez Froullé, 1788; Sowerby, vol. 3, 221-22 #3005, where she provides extensive information. On equal rights for women: vol. 1, 281-87.

[106] Kimball, 59, 82, 84-85, 116-19, 209; Wilson, 160-61.

[107] Longus, *Gli Amori Pastorali di Dafni e Cloe libri quattro descritti da Longo Greco*. Ora per la prima volta volgarizzati da Gasparo Gozzi. Venezia, 1766; Sowerby, vol. 3, 443 #4329 longer extant, no replacement copy; *Le nouveau Théatre Italien, ou Recueil General des Comédies Representées par les Comédiens Italiens Ordinaires du Roi . . Nouvelle Édition, Corrigée & tres-augmentée ...* Tome Premier [Neuvième]. A Paris, Chez Briasson, rüe Saint Jacques, à la Science. MDCCXXXIII-[MDCCXXXVI]. Avec Approbation & Privilège du Roi, Sowerby, vol. 3, 550-51, #4580.

Josaphat),[108] the former bears Jefferson's initials and several annotations.

The post-Revolutionary period of Jefferson's life brought an instance of direct contact with Venice. In 1784, at the instruction of Congress, he joined John Adams and Benjamin Franklin in writing to the Venetian Republic requesting the negotiation of a Treaty of Amity and Commerce between the two states. No response was forthcoming from Venice, which, already in its final commercial and political decline, feared both the enmity of the English and the successful revolutionary model of the Americans.[109]

---

[108] Luigi Riccoboni, *An Historical and Critical Account of the Theatres in Europe* ... London: Printed for T. Waller, in the Temple; and R. Dodsley, in Pall-Mall, 1741, Sowerby, vol. 5, 43 #4706, where she notes that Jefferson initialled it; [Johannes Damascenus], [*Vita di San Giosafat convertito da Barlaam*], Venezia, n.d. circa 1600, Sowerby, vol. 2, 132 #1552, with detailed information on the defective copy. It could be added that on A 2 'Mar tha' is written in what appears to be a youthful hand, and that a similar hand practiced writing the letter 'm' on p. 94; that 94 bears the cue word "Atto', the first word on the first leaf of the missing quire or quires; and that the text bears some signs of the dialect of the Venetian mainland, including on 17 *magagnato* ('malformed', 'wounded', 'crippled').

[109] See Federica Ambrosini, "Rapporti politici e commerciali tra Repubblica Veneta e Stati Uniti sul finire del secolo XVIII," in Piero Del Negro and Federica Ambrosini, *L'aquila e il leone* (Padua: Programma e 1+1 Editori, 1989) 29-124, esp. 76-94.

Possible Reflections of Italian Thought in that of Jefferson and His Immediate Predecessors

The review of Jefferson's Italian and Italian-related books has demonstrated that the content of a number of them had close relationships to his thinking about human individuals and human communities and how both might best live and self-govern to preserve and enhance their birthright of freedom and equality. A closer study promises to deepen understanding of his views. Because Jefferson made few explicit indications of their connection with his thinking,[110] considerations must rest chiefly on congruities that may reflect the specific texts in Jefferson's library, the long tradition of Western thinking to which they belong including his own, or both. The Declaration's famous affirmation and Jefferson's proposals for the Virginia constitution and legal system are the most relevant.

The Declaration will be cited here in the form that is the closest extant to Jefferson's original draft, the text frequently termed the "original Rough Draught."[111]

When in the course of human events it becomes necessary for a people to advance from that subordination in which they have hitherto remained, & to assume among the powers of the earth the equal & independant station to which the laws of nature & of nature's god entitle

---

[110] Cf. Kimball's intuition that Jefferson in his commonplace books took fewer notes on the works in which "he found the reflection or confirmation of his own thoughts and opinions" (244-45).

[111] Jefferson, *Papers*, 415 (Editorial Note) 423-28 (reproducing the text exactly, including idiosyncracies in spelling and punctuation).

> them ... We hold these truths to be sacred & undenia-
> ble; that all men are created equal & independant, that
> from that equal creation they derive rights inherent &
> inalienable, among which are the preservation of life, &
> liberty, & the pursuit of happiness, that to secure these
> ends, governments are instituted among men, deriving
> their just powers from the consent of the governed, that
> whenever any form of government shall become de-
> structive of these ends, it is the right of the people to al-
> ter or to abolish it, & to institute new government, laying
> it's foundation on such principles & organizing it's pow-
> ers in such form, as to them shall seem most likely to ef-
> fect their safety & happiness ...

In the Virginia Constitution of which he made multiple
drafts in the years surrounding the Declaration, Jefferson
realized his theories in governmental norms and structures that, as the editors of his papers note, he saw as being under the authority of "the sovereign people." They
go on to say that the drafts contain

> most if not all of the leading principles to which Jeffer-
> son's entire career was dedicated: the people as the
> source of authority; the protection of 'public liberty' and
> of individual rights against authoritarian control; the
> widening of suffrage and an equalization of the distribu-
> tion of representation in the legislative branch; the use
> of unappropriated lands for the establishment of a soci-
> ety of independent farmers who would hold their lands
> 'in full and absolute dominion of no superior whatever';
> the just and equitable treatment of the Indians; the use

of the western lands so as to remove friction with neigh-
boring states and promote the cause of nationality; the
encouragement of immigration and the lowering of bar-
riers to naturalization; the elevation of the civil over the
military authority; the abolition of privilege and preroga-
tive; and so on.[112]

Consistently with these views, Jefferson opens his draft with
a bill of charges against the British monarch that chiefly
concern treatment of Americans not as equals but as a sub-
jugated population, including by military force (338-39). He
proposed a separation of the three branches of government
(340) and the limitation of service to a single branch (347);
restrictions on the powers of the executive by assigning to
the legislature the general power to restrict the executive
and the veto of bills, the dissolving of the legislature, and
the declaring of war or organizing of an army (341-42); a
bicameral government consisting of a house of Representatives of a number proportional to the number of electors,
qualification as elector consisting of payment of the most
basic taxes and a brief residence, and a Senate of a fixed
number to be elected by the Representatives. Both cham-
bers would have an annual term and both could originate
bills "except that money bills shall originate with representatives."[113] He concludes with the deposing of George "by

---

[112] Jefferson, *Papers*, vol. 1, 330, editorial note, where it is observed that the first
and second drafts go much more in the direction of equalizing inheritance, of
religious freedom, and of limitations on capital punishment than the third; 329-
86 for the drafts and related material.

[113] Jefferson, *Papers*, vol. 1, 341; see also on 121-37 the 1774 "Draft of Instructions
to the Virginia Delegates in the Continental Congress" in which similar views are

the authority of the people" (356-57).

As is clear from the history of the questions presented above, Jefferson's texts unite the older strain of Stoic thought recognizing the equality of all human beings deriving from their common nature and their life work of the 'pursuit of happiness' (defined as the rational direction of the entire life in harmony with nature and the good[114] as opposed to the self-centered and momentary 'pursuit of pleasure') through self-governance. While Jefferson overtly associated the historical roots of self-government with Germanic peoples and specifically the Anglo-Saxons, perhaps to appeal to fellow colonials as their birthright from their own culture, he privately remarked upon the continuation of self-government by ancient Greeks in their colonies in southern Italy. The books that he chose for his library conveyed to him as well the fruits of the medieval communal and Conciliar development of the corporate body's right to govern itself and — in order to do so — to create structures of governance, to delegate the power of governance to specific individuals, and — finally — to reclaim that power when the specific individuals fail to achieve the community's goals or act in antipathy to them. It is from the union of notions of universal equal rights and the universal right to self-government that Jefferson's bill of particulars against George III is derived, describing actions of the king so destructive of both individual American colonials and their

advanced. In the Third Draft of the Virginia Constitution, Jefferson proposed the further limitation of government service in any branch to a single term.
[114] Colish, *Stoic Tradition*, vol. 1, 36 and see, *e.g.* Aristotle, *Nicomachaean Ethics.*

communities (plural because each colony had its own government) as to justify the communities' collective retracting of their delegation to him of their power of governance through the action of the Continental Congress.

While, as is commonly acknowledged, Jefferson's views reflect the influence of Locke, Montesquieu, and Hobbes, they also reflect, directly and indirectly, the norms of earlier European thinkers and activists, the Italian ones already described and English ones. Sir John Baker describes the deep English history of the rule of law and human rights, concluding that "it is not so absurd to propose that the rule of law was an accepted constitutional principle in the Tudor and Stuart period, and that many — though certainly not quite all — of the rights now classified as 'human rights' would have been recognized without difficulty by English lawyers of that period." He notes that by 1628 or earlier taxation could only be imposed with the consent of Parliament.[115] The separation of the three powers of government as a guarantor of liberty, according to Bernard Bailyn, "had been a popular doctrine among the extreme radicals during the Civil War" and later was favored by Locke and Montesquieu.[116] The latter cited it as practiced by the Venetian republic but criticized their drawing of officials of all three from the same body (the hereditary patriciate) as blunting

---

[115] Sir John Baker, "Human Rights and the Rule of Law in Renaissance England," *Northwestern University Journal of International Human Rights*, Special Issue "At Century's Dawn: The Past and Future of Human Rights and the Rule of Law," 2 (2004): 24-40, quotation 37.

[116] Bernard Bailyn, *Origins of American Politics* (New York: Alfred A. Knopf, 1968) 21-22.

its effect, perhaps because his constitutional theory, as interpreted by Michael Zuckert, was shaped by his concept of natural rights.[117]

Numerous English thinkers of the seventeenth century involved in the English Civil Wars espoused many similar values and included Italian works among their sources. Cited by Pocock as hostile to liberalism, the thinkers have been re-read by Vickie B. Sullivan, who, on the contrary, demonstrates their liberal republican views, according to which the person comes first and is served by the state through the preservation of personal rights.[118] Marchamon Nedham, for example, welcomed popular participation in governance as a means "of the protection of the people's individual rights" and substituted "the ancient conception of political association, expressed in Aristotle's view that a city should not only keep order but also improve the character of its citizens" with "something very close to the modern, liberal notion that politics is a means by which individuals attain security and comfort" (115). Nedham cited Machiavelli in justifying the deposing of a king who had used force to abuse his power by the governing body that

---

[117] Michael Zuckert, "Natural Rights and Modern Constitutionalism," *Northwestern University Journal of International Human Rights*, Special Issue "At Century's Dawn: The Past and Future of Human Rights and the Rule of Law," 2 (2004): 42-66.

[118] Vickie B. Sullivan, *Machiavelli, Hobbes, and the Formation of a Liberal Republicanism in England* (Cambridge: Cambridge University Press, 2004) esp. 2-8 citing the individual-based republicanism in the views of preceding English political thinkers, influenced by Machiavelli; 15-20 on the reluctance to cite Machiavelli and Hobbes by name while drawing on their thought; 121 on Machiavelli's justification of rebellion against tyranny; 127-41 on Nedham's views.

ranked immediately below him (121). He went further in later work, abandoning the notion of obedience to those in charge and affirming instead that "politics begins in a contract that establishes civil society" and "should protect individual rights to liberty and property in addition to life and that the people can and should withdraw their consent when government fails in that protection" (127-28). He emphasized freedom for all, "'wholesome laws suited to every man's state and condition'," with "'easy administration'" and the "'power of altering governments and governors upon occasion'" and advocated "'parliaments or assemblies of the people'" whose members are freely elected as necessary to the freedom and security of the people (128-29). As Sullivan concludes, "like Hobbes and later Locke, Nedham insists that 'the original and foundation of all just power and government is in the people'" (129). While acknowledging Machiavelli as a source, Nedham corrected what he considered inapplicable or incorrect views in the Italian thinker's works, especially by affirming the right of the people to participate in all functions of government (130-39), to punish rulers who commit misdeeds (141), and to participate in the conflict that is a natural part of a system emphasizing individual freedom (141).

James Harrington, another thinker involved in the English Civil Wars and whom Kevin Hayes sees as influencing Jefferson in the period before the Declaration of Independence,[119] sought to avoid the dependence of good gov-

---

[119] Hayes, 264.

ernment on personal virtue by devising a two-chamber system. It was composed of a senate drawn from the wealthier of two classes of landowners and a popular assembly from the less wealthy one. In his view, the senate would utilize the highly developed capacities of the social elite, while the assembly would more effectively promote the interests of the broader populace; the result would be the good governance of all (Sullivan, 181). The influence of Machiavelli on Harrington, who repeatedly cites him, is widely recognized (esp. 156-59). However, his criticism of the Venetians for excluding the people from governance and defense (158) seems to have distracted scholars from the much greater congruity of Harrington's proposals with the Venetian model than with the Florentine thinker's. Beyond the Venetian secret ballot that Sullivan notes (151), the two-chamber system itself seems an adaptation of Venice's Senate and Maggior Consiglio. The Maggior Consiglio was by far the broadest-based governing body in the Italian republican (or any other Western governing) tradition; the entire and relatively large patriciate, frequently numbering over 2,000 individuals, belonged to it by birth and for life. It elected members to the Senate and had final authority over various matters that might originate in the Senate, including the election of all offices and final decisions over the punishment of crimes.[120] It should be noted that in Jefferson's system the severe limits on the

---

[120] Giuseppe Cappelletti, *Relazione storica sulle magistrature venete* (Venice: Grimaldo, 1873; repr. Venice: Filippi, 1992) esp. 26-36.

executive branch and the powers assigned to the legislative branch, such as authority over the military, closely follow the Venetian model, including the deciding of certain issues of great consequence to all by its lower body. Other features of Harrington's system were common to the Italian communes including Florence: limited terms for those elected, the requirement that at its conclusion the member sit out for a designated period, and the equal division of inheritance among all brothers. The influence of both Machiavelli and the Venetian model is apparent also in the work of Henry Neville, who, after his incarceration for his participation in the English republican movement, moved to Italy. His translation of Machiavelli's works was published in 1675, prefaced by a letter to Zanobi Buondelmonti justifying actions purported to be by Machiavelli but that Neville himself is believed to have written (Sullivan, 187). Neville's *Plato Redivivus* concerning an English gentleman, his Venetian visitor, and an English doctor expresses political views that "clearly draw an equation between the human body and the body politic" (177).

Finally, Algernon Sidney, long recognized as providing important inspiration to the American colonials including Jefferson, as Jefferson himself acknowledged (Sullivan, 200-201), supported republics and opposed monarchy to the point that he was "executed in 1683 for his purported involvement in the Rye House Plot" (200). His republicanism, which is based on passion and the controlled use of power rather than reason, derives from

Machiavelli's, a source that has been overlooked because of the paucity of named citations (cf. 201-13). Sidney saw those who rule as doing so only with the consent of the people, who are empowered to judge them on their performance; that all men are born equal and free and that therefore no man has a birthright to rule over others (218-23); and that the people have a right to resist aggressive rulers, even with arms (223-24).

Concluding Summary

The concept of human equality was developed by Stoics in the classical period and furthered through the substitution of descending authority with ascending authority by the communal and conciliar movements in Italy in the transition from the Middle Ages to the Renaissance. Padua claims a prominent (and currently under-recognized) role in the developments through its preservation of Aristotle's works and scientific approach, combined with its early and strong broad-based governing tradition, separation of secular and ecclesiastical powers, leadership in the conciliar movement, and artistic and literary traditions. After a period of absolutism, European and American activists of the seventeenth and eighteenth centuries reprised the earlier developments, the texts of the earlier movements occupying an important role in their thinking.

Moreover, the economic dynamic that generated the movements in the political sphere generated a congruent change in the cultural sphere, as described by Victor Turner in a fundamental essay.[121] Turner describes how with the shifting of societies' crucial economic source from agriculture, based on a fixed annual cycle of repeated actions and limited profits, to trade and proto-manufacturing, based on boundless creativity and with potentially extremely high profits, the role and content of the performative arts underwent a similar shift. In the earlier phase, they formed

---

[121] Victor Turner, "From Liminal to Liminoid in Play, Flow, and Ritual: An Essay in Comparative Symbology," now in *From Ritual to Theatre. The Human Seriousness of Play* (New York: Performance Arts Journal Publications, 1982) 20-60.

part of a closed and repetitious system congruent with the annual crop cycle and thus were permitted during brief, defined periods such as Carnival and in designated (often marginal) spaces with the purpose of relieving the social pressures generated by a fixed and hierarchical social authority and limited financial resources. At the end of the designated period, the social classes resumed their appointed, enduring roles. This phase was termed 'liminal' by Turner. With the development of proto-manufacturing and trade, the creative arts were freed from the structured annual cycle to become a constant part of social life in both timing and location; the creative process was unleashed from bondage to top-down social authority. Turner termed this phase 'liminoid'. As he recognized, the shift first occurred in Italy in the late Middle Ages, as several major cities including Venice and Florence turned to proto-manufacturing and international commerce. Boccaccio's *Decameron* was identified as at the leading edge of the literary development by Joy Potter.[122] It is thus not by chance that Ghismonda's statement of human equality, made at a time when the Italian communes and the Council of cardinals developed their views of rights and self-governing systems, bears a strong resemblance to Jefferson's. In early-sixteenth-century Italy, the unusual openness consequent upon the damage inflicted on social authority struc-

---

[122] Joy H. Potter, *Five Frames for the* Decameron (Princeton: Princeton University Press, 1982); see also Linda L. Carroll, "Authorial Defense in Boccaccio and Ruzante: From Liminal to Liminoid," *Romance Quarterly* (formerly *Kentucky Romance Quarterly*) 34 (1987): 103-16.

tures by the international wars allowed daring theatrical writers — Bernardo Bibbiena, Ludovico Ariosto and Angelo Beolco among them — to affirm through their characters the intelligence and talents of women, servants, and peasants, implicitly or explicitly raising them to the level of hegemonic males at least in certain situations.[123] The early seventeenth century brought perhaps the most glorious Italian articulation of rights in the work of Paolo Sarpi and Galileo Galilei. It was also their final flourishing, to be followed by the cultural and intellectual liddedness of Italy's reinfeudalization subsequent to the loss of commerce, which had shifted to the Atlantic, and the imposition of a strict descending system by civic and ecclesiastical authorities.

When, in the colonies that the Veneto mariner Giovanni Caboto had assisted the English in finding, Jefferson addressed these issues, he developed views expressed by the participants in the English Civil Wars and Glorious Revolution and by the heir of the communal and Conciliar traditions, Paolo Sarpi. Furthering the parallelism between the human body and the body politic, Jefferson proclaimed first the rights and faculties of each human person and then the same rights and faculties for communities of human persons. In so doing, he solved the question of whether individual or communal rights should prevail in the struc-

---

[123] See Linda L. Carroll, "Carnival Rites as Vehicles of Protest in Renaissance Venice," *Sixteenth Century Journal* 15 (1985): 487-502; *ead.*, "Authorial Defense"; *ead.*, "Who's on Top?: Gender as Societal Power Configuration," *Sixteenth Century Journal* 20 (1989): 531-58; *ead.*, "Dating *The Woman from Ancona*," *Sixteenth Century Journal* 31 (2000): 963-85.

ture and actions of government. One could note in this also the potential influence of Sarpi's thought according to which the civic community's right to self-determination in the face of the exertion of authority by an external body parallels that of the individual Christian exercising free will in making ethical choices in the face of ecclesiastical authorities.

The driving role of economic factors recognized by Turner in the turn to liminoid at the beginning of the modern period has recently been discerned by Steven Pincus in the Glorious Revolution and in the American move to independence as well.[124] Pincus's research on vast quantities of primary materials adds to Turner's insight by identifying trade as crucial to the success of revolutions in creating democracies because of its requirement of freedom of information, action, and movement.

> Merchant communities demand free flows of information to conduct their trade and are thus hostile to authoritarian regimes that monopolize information. It was the economic and political clout of the foreign trading communities, I suspect, that prevented England after 1688 and the United States in the early national period from adopting one-party rule.

It is therefore no accident that Jefferson and the other independence-minded colonials put the unfettered exercise of commerce at the center of their concerns.

---

[124] Steven Pincus, *1688: The First Modern Revolution* (New Haven: Yale University Press, 2009) 44; *id.*, *The Heart of the Declaration. The Founders' Case for an Activist Government* (New Haven: Yale University Press, 2016).

BIBLIOGRAPHY

Primary Works

Amelot de La Houssaye, Abraham-Nicholas. 1762. "Translator's Preface." In *The Works of Nicholas Machiavel, Secretary of State to the Republic of Florence*. Trans. and ed. Ellis Farneworth. 2 vols. London: Thomas Davies, Thomas Waller, R. and J. Dodsley, James Fletcher; Edinburgh: Balfour and Hamilton; Dublin: James Hoey Junior. 1: 496-502

Anonymous. [1678]. *Examen de la Liberté originaire de Venise. Traduit de l'Italien. Avec une harangue de Louis Hélian contre les Venetiens, traduit du Latin*. Trans. Abraham-Nicholas Amelot de La Houssaye. [Ratisbonne?: Jean Aubri].

Anonymous, ed. 1732. *The Cases of Polygamy, Adultery, Concubinage, Divorce, etc. Seriously and Learnedly Discussed. Being a Compleat Collection of all the Remarkable Tryals and Tracts which have been Written on those Important Subjects By the most Eminent Hands*. London: Printed for T. Payne, in Pater-Noster Row; J. Chrichley, at Charing-Cross; and W. Shropshire, in New-Bond Street.

Anonymous. 1760. *Memoria inedita presentata al Senato Veneto dal celebre Fra Paolo Sarpi Intorno al modo da tenersi dalla Repubblica per il buono e durevol governo del suo Stato*. Colonia [but Livorno?]: Pietro Mortier.

Beccaria, Cesare. 1809. *An Essay on crimes & punishments*, translated from the Italian. With a commentary, attributed to M. de Voltaire. Translated from the French...New York: Stephen Gould.

Beolco, Angelo (Il Ruzante). 1967. *Teatro*. Ed. and trans. Ludovico Zorzi. Turin: Einaudi.

_____. *La prima oratione*. 2009. Ed. and trans. Linda L. Carroll. MHRA Critical Texts Vol. 16. London: Modern Humanities Research Association.

Boccaccio, Giovanni. 1976. *Decameron*. Ed. Vittore Branca. *Tutte le opere*, vol. 4. Milan: Mondadori.

Buommattei, Benedetto. 1735. *Della lingua Toscana di Benedetto Buommatei.* Venice.

Farneworth, Ellis. 1762. "Advertisement to the Reader." In *The Works of Nicholas Machiavel, Secretary of State to the Republic of Florence.* Trans. and ed. Ellis Farneworth. 2 vols. London: Thomas Davies, Thomas Waller, R. and J. Dodsley, James Fletcher; Edinburgh: Balfour and Hamilton; Dublin: James Hoey Junior. 1: xiii-xvi; 2: v-viii.

Galilei, Galileo. 1744. *Opere di Galileo Galilei divise in quattro tomi, In questa nuova Edizione accresciute di molte cose inedite* ... New edition. 4 vols. Padua: Nella Stamperia del Seminario. Appresso Gio: Manfrè.

_____. 1976. *Galileo Against the Philosophers in His* Dialogue of Cecco di Ronchitti *(1605) and* Considerations of Alimberto Mauri *(1606) in English Translations.* Ed. and trans. Stillman Drake. Los Angeles: Zeitlin and Ver Brugge.

Garzoni, Pietro. 1738-39. "Riflessioni del N.H. f. Pietro Garzoni sopra il Guicciardini." In Francesco Guicciardini. *Istoria d'Italia.* 2 vols. Venice: Giambattista Pasquali. Unnumbered front matter.

Griselini, Francesco. 1760. *Memorie anedote spettanti alla Vita ed agli studj del sommo Filosofo e Giureconsulto F. Paolo Sarpi Servita raccolte ed ordinate da Francesco Griselini Veneziano, della celebre Accademia dell'Istituto delle Scienze di Bologna.* 2nd ed. Lausanne: Giovanni Nestenus and Company.

Jefferson, Thomas. "1762-1767, Legal Commonplace Book," Library of Congress, The Thomas Jefferson Papers at the Library of Congress, Manuscript Division, Series 5, Commonplace Books, Microfilm Reel 059, http://hdl.loc.gov/loc.mss/mtj.mtjbib026466.

_____ 1950-. *The Papers of Thomas Jefferson.* Ed. Julian P. Boyd (Editor), Lyman H. Butterfield and Mina R. Bryan (Associate Editors). Princeton: Princeton University Press.

_____. 1989. *Jefferson's Literary Commonplace Book*. Ed. Douglas L. Wilson. The Papers of Thomas Jefferson, Second Series. Princeton: Princeton University Press.

_____. 1997. *Jefferson's Memorandum Books, Accounts, with Legal Records and Miscellany 1767-1826*. Ed. James A. Bear, Jr. and Lucia C. Stanton. 2 vols. Princeton: Princeton University Press.

[Johannes Damascenus]. *ca.* 1600. [*Vita di San Giosafat convertito da Barlaam*]. Venice.

Limojon de St. Didier, Alexandre Toussaint. 1680. *La ville et la république de Venise*. Paris: Guillaume de Luyne.

Lucian of Samosata. 1563. *Luciani opera*. Ed. Gilbert Cousin, János Zsámboki, and Jakob Zwinger. 4 vols. Basel: Sebastianus Henricuspetrus.

_____. 1664. *Lucien*. Trans. Nicolas Perrot d'Ablancourt. 4th ed. revised. 2 vols. Amsterdam: Jean de Ravestein.

_____. 1743. *Luciani Samosatensis opera*. Ed. Tiberius Hemsterhuis, Johann Matthias Gesner, Johan Frederik Reitz, and Jean Brodin. 3 vols. Amsterdam: Jacobus Wetstenius.

Mazzei, Philip (Filippo). 1768. *A Letter on the behaviour of the populace on a late occasion, in the procedure against a noble lord. Lettera Intorno al Comportamento Del Popolo Inglese In un fatto seguito ultimamente Contro un signore*. 2nd Edition. London: W. Bingle.

_____. 1788. *Recherches historiques et Politiques sur les É. U. de l'Amérique Septentrionale* ... Première [-Quatrième] partie. Paris: A. Colle.

_____. 1942. *Memoirs of the Life and Peregrinations of the Florentine Philip Mazzei 1730-1816*. Trans. and ed. Howard R. Marraro. New York: Columbia University Press.

_____. 1949. "Philip Mazzei on American Political, Social, and Economic Problems." Trans. and ed. Howard R. Marraro. *The Journal of Southern History* 15: 354-78.

_____. 1983. *Philip Mazzei Selected Writings and Correspondence*. Trans. and ed. Margherita Marchione, Stanley

J. Idzerda, and S. Eugene Scalia. 3 vols. Prato: Edizioni del Palazzo.

Ochino, Bernardino. 1732. *On Polygamy. A Dialogue.* In *The Cases of Polygamy, Adultery, Concubinage, Divorce, etc. Seriously and Learnedly Discussed. Being a Compleat Collection of all the Remarkable Tryals and Tracts which have been Written on those Important Subjects By the most Eminent Hands.* London: T. Payne, J. Chrichley, and W. Shropshire. 1-65.

Sarpi, Paolo. 1974. *Istoria del Concilio Tridentino.* Ed. Corrado Vivanti. 2 vols. Turin: Giulio Einaudi.

Verri, Pietro. 1771. *Meditazioni sulla economia politica.* Genoa: Ivone Gravier and Adamo Scionico.

Voltaire. 1766. *Commentaire sur le livre des délits et des peines, par un avocat de Province.* [Geneva: No printer].

_____. 1996. *Anti-Machiavel.* Ed. Werner Bahner and Helga Bergmann. *The Complete Works of Voltaire*, vol. 19. Oxford: Voltaire Foundation.

Secondary Works

Ambrosini, Federica. 1989. "Rapporti politici e commerciali tra Repubblica Veneta e Stati Uniti sul finire del secolo XVIII." In Piero Del Negro and Federica Ambrosini. *L'aquila e il leone.* Padua: Programma e 1+1 Editori. 29-124.

Bailyn, Bernard. 1967. *Ideological Origins of the American Revolution.* Cambridge and London: The Belknap Press of Harvard University Press. 1967.

_____. 1968. *Origins of American Politics.* New York: Alfred A. Knopf.

Baker, Sir John. 2004. "Human Rights and the Rule of Law in Renaissance England." *Northwestern University Journal of International Human Rights.* Special Issue "At Century's Dawn: The Past and Future of Human Rights and the Rule of Law." 2: 24-40.

Basile, Giuseppe. 2002. "Giotto's Pictorial Cycle." In *Giotto. The Frescoes of the Scrovegni Chapel in Padua.* Ed.

Giuseppe Basile. Milan: Skira; Rome: Istituto Centrale per il Restauro. 21-39.

Beltramini, Guido. 2015. "Jefferson and Palladio." In *Jefferson and Palladio. Constructing a New World*, Centro Internazionale di Studi di Architettura Andrea Palladio, exh. cat. Vicenza, Palladio Museum 19 September 2015 - 28 March 2016. Vicenza: Centro Internazionale di Studi di Architettura Andrea Palladio; Milan: Officina Libraria. 21-37.

Bessler, John D. 2018. *The Celebrated Marquis. An Italian Noble and the Making of the Modern World*. Durham, NC: Carolina Academic Press.

Bouwsma, William J. 1968. *Venice and the Defense of Republican Liberty*. Berkeley and Los Angeles: University of California Press.

Branham, R. Bracht. 1985. "Utopian Laughter: Lucian and Thomas More." *Moreana* 86: 23-43.

_____. 1989. *Unruly Eloquence. Lucian and the Comedy of Traditions*. Revealing Antiquity 2. Cambridge: Harvard University Press.

Breidenbach, Michael D. 2016. "Conciliarism and the American Founding." *William and Mary Quarterly*, 3rd ser. 73: 467-500.

Cappelletti, Giuseppe. *Relazione storica sulle magistrature venete*. 1873/1992. Venice: Grimaldo; Venice: Filippi.

Carroll, Linda L. 1987. "Authorial Defense in Boccaccio and Ruzante: From Liminal to Liminoid." *Romance Quarterly* 34: 103-16.

_____. 1985. "Carnival Rites as Vehincles of Protest in Renaissance Venice," *Sixteenth Century Journal*. 16: 487-502.

_____. 2000. "Dating The Woman from Ancona," *Sixteenth Century Journal*. 31: 963-85

_____. 1989. "Who's on Top?: Gender as Societal Power Configuration." *Sixteenth Century Journal*. 20: 531-58.

Certeau, Michel de. 1984. *The Practice of Everyday Life*. Trans. Steven F. Rendall. Berkeley and Los Angeles: University of California Press.

Checchini, Aldo. 1909. "Comuni rurali padovani." *Nuovo Archivio Veneto*. n.s. 18: 131-84.

Colbourn, H. Trevor. 1958. "Thomas Jefferson's Use of the Past." *The William and Mary Quarterly*, 3rd series 15: 56-70.

Colish, Marcia L. 1985. *The Stoic Tradition from Antiquity to the Early Middle Ages*. 2 vols. Leiden: Brill.

————. 1999. *Medieval Foundations of the Western Tradition*. New Haven: Yale University Press.

Cozzi, Gaetano. 1956. "Fra Paolo Sarpi, l'anglicanesimo e la *Historia del Concilio Tridentino*." *Rivista storica italiana*. 63: 559-619.

————. 1978. *Paolo Sarpi tra Venezia e l'Europa*. Turin: Einaudi.

Dionisotti, Carlo. 1980. "La testimonianza del Brucioli." In *Machiavellerie*. Einaudi paperbacks 113. Turin: Einaudi. 193-226.

Ferrante, Joan M. 1975. *Woman as Image in Medieval Literature*. New York and London: Columbia University Press.

Gilreath, James and Douglas L. Wilson, eds. 1989. *Thomas Jefferson's Library*. A Catalog with the Entries in His Own Order. Washington, D.C.: Library of Congress.

Gullino, Giuseppe. 1999. "Garzoni, Pietro." *Dizionario Biografico degli Italiani*. 52.

Hayes, Kevin J. 2008. *The Road to Monticello. The Life and Mind of Thomas Jefferson*. New York: Oxford University Press.

Heller, Wendy. 2003. *Emblems of Eloquence. Opera and Women's Voices in Seventeenth-Century Venice*. Berkeley and London: University of California Press.

Kimball, Marie. 1943. *Jefferson The Road to Glory 1773 to 1776*. New York: Coward-McCann.

Koch, Adrienne. 1961. "Jefferson and the Pursuit of Happiness." In *Power, Morals, and the Founding Fathers*. Ithaca: Cornell University Press. 23-49.

Lawrence, Jason. 2005. *'Who the devil taught thee so much Italian?' Italian Language Learning and Literary Imitation in Early Modern England*. Manchester and New York: Manchester University Press

Lehmann, Karl. 1965. *Thomas Jefferson American Humanist*. Chicago: University of Chicago Press.

Lovarini, Emilio. 1965a. "Galileo interprete del Ruzzante." In *Studi sul Ruzzante e sulla letteratura pavana*. Ed. Gianfranco Folena. Padua: Antenore. 377-92.

_____. 1965b. "Galileo scrittore pavano?". In *Studi*. 391-410.

Madden, Thomas F. 2003. *Enrico Dandolo and the Rise of Venice*. Baltimore: The Johns Hopkins University Press.

Miller, Charles A. 1988. *Jefferson and Nature: An Interpretation* (Baltimore: The Johns Hopkins University Press.

Muir, Edward. 2007. *Culture Wars of the Late Renaissance: Skeptics, Libertines, and Opera*. Cambridge: Harvard University Press.

Mullett, Charles F. 1939. "Classical Influences on the American Revolution" *The Classical Journal* 35: 92-104.

Ní Chuilleanáin, Eiléan. 2007. "Motives of translation: More, Erasmus and Lucian" *Hermathena* 183: 49-62.

Oakley, Francis. 1971. "The 'New Conciliarism' and Its Implications: A Problem in History and Hermeneutics." *Journal of Ecumenical Studies*. 8: 815-40.

_____. 1972. "Conciliarism at the Fifth Lateran Council?" *Church History*. 41: 452-63.

_____. 1982. "Religious and Ecclesiastical Life on the Eve of the Reformation." In *Reformation Europe: A Guide to Research*. Ed. Steven Ozment. St. Louis: Center for Reformation Research. 5-32.

Piaia, Gregorio. 1977. *Marsilio da Padova nella Riforma e nella Controriforma. Fortuna ed interpretazione*. Padua: Antenore.

BIBLIOGRAPHY

Pincus, Steven. 2009. *1688: The First Modern Revolution*. New Haven: Yale University Press.

————. 2016. *The Heart of the Declaration. The Founders' Case for an Activist Government*. New Haven: Yale University Press.

Pocock, J. G. A. 2003. *The Machiavellian Moment. Florentine Political Thought and the Atlantic Republican Tradition*. 2nd paperback ed. with a new afterward by the author. Princeton: Princeton University Press.

Potter, Joy H. 1982. *Five Frames for the* Decameron. Princeton: Princeton University Press.

Rebel, Hermann. 1982. *Peasant Classes. The Bureaucratization of Property and Family Relations Under Early Hapsburg Absolutism 1511-1636*. Princeton: Princeton University Press.

Ridley, Jasper. 1982. *The Statesman and the Fanatic. Thomas Wolsey and Thomas More*. London: Constable.

Riverso, Nicla. 2016. "Paolo Sarpi: The Hunted Friar and his Popularity in England." In *Speaking Truth to Power from Medieval to Modern Italy*. Ed. Jo Ann Cavallo and Carlo Lottieri. *Annali d'Italianistica* 34: 297-318.

Robinson, Christopher. 1979. *Lucian and His Influence in Europe*. Chapel Hill: The University of North Carolina Press.

Rosand, Ellen. 1991. *Opera in Seventeenth-Century Venice: The Creation of a Genre*. Berkeley and London: University of California Press.

Saccenti, Riccardo. 2016. *Debating Medieval Natural Law. A Survey*. Notre Dame: University of Notre Dame Press.

Sanesi, Ireneo. 1954. *La commedia*. 2 vols. Milan: Vallardi.

Sanford, Charles B. 1977. *Jefferson and His Library*. Hamden, CT: Archon Books.

Schlegel, Ursula. 1969. "On the Pictorial Program of the Arena Chapel." In *Giotto: The Arena Chapel Frescoes*. Ed. James Stubblebine. New York: Norton. 182-202.

Setton, Kenneth M. *The Sixteenth Century to the Reign of Julius III*. vol. 3 of *The Papacy and the Levant (1204-*

1571). Memoirs of the American Philosophical Society, vol. 161. Philadelphia: The American Philosophical Society.

Shorr, Dorothy C. 1969. "The Role of the Virgin in Giotto's *Last Judgment.*" In *Giotto: The Arena Chapel Frescoes.* Ed. James Stubblebine. New York: Norton. 169-82.

Skinner, Quentin. 1988. "Political Philosophy." In *The Cambridge History of Renaissance Philosophy.* Ed. Charles B. Schmitt and Quentin Skinner. Cambridge: Cambridge University Press. 389-452.

Soll, Jacob. 2008. *Publishing* The Prince. *History, Reading, and the Birth of Political Criticism.* Ann Arbor: University of Michigan Press.

Sowerby, E. Millicent. 1952. *Catalogue of the Library of Thomas Jefferson.* 5 vols. Washington: The Library of Congress.

Sullivan, Vickie B. 2004. *Machiavelli, Hobbes, and the Formation of a Liberal Republicanism in England.* Cambridge: Cambridge University Press.

Surtz, Edward S.J. 1957a. *The Praise of Pleasure. Philosophy, Education, and Communism in More's* Utopia. Cambridge: Harvard University Press.

_____. 1957b. *The Praise of Wisdom. A Commentary on the Religious and Moral Problems and Backgrounds of St. Thomas More's* Utopia. Chicago: Loyola University Press.

Tierney, Brian. 1955. "Franciscus Zabarella." In *Foundations of Conciliar Theory.* Cambridge: Cambridge University Press. 220-37.

_____. 1980. "Public expediency and natural law: a fourteenth-century discussion on the origins of government and property." In *Authority and Power: Studies on Medieval Law and Government Presented to Walter Ullmann on his Seventieth Birthday.* Ed. Brian Tierney and Peter Linehan. Cambridge: Cambridge University Press. 167-82.

_____. 1989. "Origins of Natural Rights Language: Texts and Contexts, 1150-1250." *History of Political Thought.* 10: 615-46.

_____. 1997. *The Idea of Natural Rights.* Atlanta: Scholar's Press for Emory University.

Tortarolo, Edoardo. 1986. *Illuminismo e Rivoluzione: Biografia politica di Filippo Mazzei.* Milan: Franco Angeli.

Turner, Victor. 1982. "From Liminal to Liminoid in Play, Flow, and Ritual: An Essay in Comparative Symbology." In *From Ritual to Theatre. The Human Seriousness of Play.* New York: Performance Arts Journal Publications. 20-60.

Valsania, Maurizio. 2017. *Jefferson's Body. A Corporeal Biography.* Charlottesville: University of Virginia Press.

Vivanti, Corrado. 1974a. "Introduzione." In Sarpi. 1: XXIX-XCII.

_____. 1974b. "Cronologia per la *Istoria del Concilio Tridentino* (1500-64) e per la vita di Paolo Sarpi (1552-1623)." In Sarpi. 1: XCIX-CLX.

Wegemer, Gerard. 2011. *Young Thomas More and the Arts of Liberty.* Cambridge: Cambridge University Press.

Wills, Garry. 1978. *Inventing America. Jefferson's Declaration of Independence.* Garden City, NY: Doubleday.

Wilson, Douglas L. 1986. "Jefferson's Library." In *Thomas Jefferson: A Reference Biography.* Ed. Merrill D. Peterson. New York: Charles Scribner's Sons. 157-79.

Wootton, David. 1983. *Paolo Sarpi.* Cambridge: Cambridge University Press.

_____. 2010. *Galileo: Watcher of the Skies.* New Haven: Yale University Press.

Zuckert, Michael. 2004. "Natural Rights and Modern Constitutionalism." In *Northwestern University Journal of International Human Rights.* Special Issue "At Century's Dawn: The Past and Future of Human Rights and the Rule of Law." 2: 42-66.

ABOUT THE AUTHOR

Linda L. Carroll is Professor Emerita of Italian at Tulane University. In her research she examines the dynamic interaction of regional language and culture with economic, social, and political factors, especially in northern Italy in the Renaissance and Enlightenment and with regard to egalitarian thought. In her most recent book, *Commerce, Peace and the Arts in Renaissance Venice. Ruzante and the Empire at Center Stage* (London: Routledge, 2016), she utilizes extensive new primary documentation to articulate the economic and political interests connecting patrons of art works in Venice's Basilica of the Frari and their relationship to the Beolco family, including the playwright Angelo (Il Ruzante) and his performances in Venice. She edited and translated Angelo Beolco (Il Ruzante), *La prima oratione* (London: Modern Humanities Research Association, 2009) and served as translator for *Venice, Città Excelentissima: Selections from the Renaissance Diaries of Marin Sanudo*, Patricia H. Labalme and Laura Sanguineti White, editors (Baltimore: The Johns Hopkins University Press, 2008). Together with Melanie L. Marshall and Katherine A. McIver, she co-edited *Sexualities, Textualities, Art and Music in Early Modern Italy. Playing with Boundaries* (Burlington, VT: Ashgate, 2014; Paperbacks Direct 2018). With Anthony M. Cummings, Zachary W. Jones, and Philip Weller, she co-edited Antonio Molino (Il Burchiella), *I Dilettevoli Madrigali a Quattro Voci [Delightful Madrigals for Four Voices..., Newly...Composed and Brought to Light...First Book...1568]* (Rome: Istituto Italiano per la Storia della Musica, 2014) and with Anthony M. Cummings and Alexander Dean, she co-edited *Don Michele Pesenti da Verona. An Edition of the Complete Works* (Middleton, WI: A-R Editions, 2019). Her numerous articles and reviews have appeared in journals including *Sixteenth Century Journal, Renaissance Quarterly, Annali d'Italianistica, MLN, Ateneo Veneto*, and *Modern Language Review* and her essays on Giorgione's *Tempest* as astrological figure, Machiavelli's Veronese prostitute, speaking truth to power, irreverence in the Renaissance, the conditions of Renaissance women's lives, the Turkish threat in the Renaissance, and an anthropological analysis of Luigi Pirandello's *La giara* (The Jar) have appeared in numerous edited volumes and conference proceedings.

ROBERT VISCUSI

—1941-2020—

Robert Viscusi was fundamental to the development of Bordighera Press; to its journal *VIA*: *Voices in Italian Americana* and to the book series *VIA* FOLIOS.

One of his many ground-breaking articles, "Breaking the Silence: Strategic Imperatives for Italian American Culture," opened *VIA*'s inaugural issue. In like fashion, his keenly satiric, genial long poem, "An Oration upon the Most Recent Death of Christopher Columbus," was the stimulus for the founding of our first book series, *VIA* FOLIOS.

In later years we also published his epic poem, *Ellis Island*, a collection of sonnets whose "Star Review" from *Publishers Weekly* concluded: "[T]he sonnets are far from uniform, at times manifesting as short stories, at other times as short bursts of philosophical inquiry or bursts of pure song. This is a new delicacy for aficionados of creative poetry and an anthem of sorts for those who—however far removed from immigration—occasionally feel displaced from home."

www.ingramcontent.com/pod-product-compliance
Lightning Source LLC
Chambersburg PA
CBHW032046040426
42449CB00007B/1000